ENGAGED LANGUAGE POLICY AND PRACTICES

Engaged Language Policy and Practices re-envisions language policy and planning as an engaged approach, drawing on and portraying theoretical and educational equity perspectives. It calls for the right to language policy-making in which all concerned—communities, parents, students, educators, and advocates—collectively imagine new strategies for resisting global neoliberal marginalization of home languages and cultural identities. This book subsequently emphasizes the means by which engaged dialectic processes can inform and clarify language policy-making decisions that promote equity. In other words, rather than descriptions of outcomes, the authors emphasize the need to detail the means by which local/regional actors resist and transform inequitable policies. These descriptions of processes thereby provide all actors with ideological, pedagogical, and equity policy tools that can inform situated school and community policy-making.

This book depicts ways in which engaged language policy embodies the intersection of critical inquiry, participant involvement, and ongoing engaged language planning processes. It further offers an alternative to the traditional top-down approach to language education policy-making. *Engaged Language Policy and Practices* is essential reading for scholars, teachers, students, communities, and others concerned with worldwide language and identity equity.

Kathryn A. Davis is Professor of Language Policies and Practices at the University of Hawai'i, USA. She is on the editorial board of the *Journal of Language, Identity, and Education*.

Prem Phyak is Lecturer at the Department of English Education at Tribhuvan University, Kirtipur, Nepal.

"This book is truly transformational. It completely changes our traditional understandings of language policy, ways to study it, and engage with it. By focusing on the ways in which subaltern counterpublics resist and transform inequitable policies handed down by states, and not simply on the outcomes of the policies themselves, Davis and Phyak revolutionize the field. The book not only provides readers with new theoretical understandings, but also with innovative ways of studying issues, discovering alternative realities, and supporting the sustained efforts of language minoritized communities to engage in shaping equitable language policies."

Ofelia García, The Graduate Center at City University of New York, USA

"Focusing on engagement, activism, and empowerment, the authors offer vivid ethnographic accounts of how engaged research in language policy and practice can make a difference in the real world. I highly recommend this book."

Angel M. Y. Lin, The University of Hong Kong

ENGAGED LANGUAGE POLICY AND PRACTICES

Kathryn A. Davis and Prem Phyak

NEW YORK AND LONDON

First published 2017
by Routledge
711 Third Avenue, New York, NY 10017

and by Routledge
2 Park Square, Milton Park, Abingdon, Oxon, OX14 4RN

Routledge is an imprint of the Taylor & Francis Group, an informa business

© 2017 Taylor & Francis

The right of Kathryn A. Davis and Prem Phyak to be identified as authors of this work has been asserted by them in accordance with sections 77 and 78 of the Copyright, Designs and Patents Act 1988.

All rights reserved. No part of this book may be reprinted or reproduced or utilised in any form or by any electronic, mechanical, or other means, now known or hereafter invented, including photocopying and recording, or in any information storage or retrieval system, without permission in writing from the publishers.

Trademark notice: Product or corporate names may be trademarks or registered trademarks, and are used only for identification and explanation without intent to infringe.

Library of Congress Cataloging in Publication Data
Names: Davis, Kathryn Anne, author. | Phyak, Prem, 1980- author.
Title: Engaged language policy and practices / Kathryn A. Davis, Prem Phyak.
Description: New York, NY : Routledge, [2017] | Includes bibliographical references.
Identifiers: LCCN 2016028210| ISBN 9781138906945 (hardback) | ISBN 9781138906952 (pbk.) | ISBN 9781317442486 (epub) | ISBN 9781317442479 (mobipocket/kindle)
Subjects: LCSH: Language policy--Political aspects. | Language planning--Political aspects. | Language and languages--Political aspects. | Intercultural communication. | Language and culture. | Sociolinguistics.
Classification: LCC P119.3 .D28 2017 | DDC 306.44/9--dc23
C record available at https://lccn.loc.gov/2016028210

ISBN: 978-1-138-90694-5 (hbk)
ISBN: 978-1-138-90695-2 (pbk)
ISBN: 978-1-315-69528-0 (ebk)

Typeset in Bembo
by HWA Text and Data Management, London

CONTENTS

Acknowledgements   *vi*

1 Introduction   1

2 Language Policies and Ideological Analyses   14

3 Engaged Ethnography as Transformative Language Policy Processes   39

4 Planning Resistance and Discovering Alternatives   58

5 Developing Relevant and Engaging Language Policies and Practices   80

6 Afterword   107

References   *114*

Index   *134*

ACKNOWLEDGMENTS

Many scholars and communities have contributed, directly or indirectly, to our conceptualization of an engaged language policy and practices approach. Teachers, youth, parents, and students have been at the forefront of informing interdisciplinary and multilingual dialogue, particularly through our work in Nepal and Hawai'i. These and other global models of engagement in language and human welfare have subsequently offered an array of possibilities for situated and equitable language policy-making.

A number of language scholars have further encouraged our engaged efforts while providing much needed social, political, and pedagogical insights that inform this book. Elana Shohamy's critical language policy perspectives have been a source of inspiration. In addition, as editors of the *Language Policy* journal, Elana Shohamy and Kendall King helped further our thinking through supporting a special issue on Engaged Language Policies and Practices (Vol. 13/2). We also express our deep respect and gratitude to those who have led the way in recognizing the political as personal in language policy and education arenas. In particular, we recognize the contributions of Suresh Canagarajah, Michelle Fine, Ofelia García, David Gegeo, Karen Watson-Gegeo, Rosemary Henze, Angel Lin, Teresa McCarty, and especially James W. Tollefson. The work of these and other scholars has encouraged us to take on this exploration of possibilities for global engaged perspectives in language policy-making.

We are also grateful to University of Hawai'i student participants in Kathryn Davis's seminar courses on engaged ethnography and language policy. We particularly appreciate Elisapeta Alaimaleata, Samuel Aguirre, Emily Gazda, Jennifer Holdway, and Lucas Edmond for their comments on earlier drafts of our book chapters. We have also received constructive feedback from scholars around the globe who attended our sessions on engaged language policy at *American Anthropological Association* and *American Association for Applied Linguistics* conferences. We are grateful to all. We further acknowledge authors whose ideas have been used in the book and Routledge editors Rebecca Novack and Kathrene Binag for their helpful advice, ongoing support, and trust that we would finish the book. We now look forward to continued engaged discussion toward supporting the people's right to language policy-making.

Mahalo and Nogen
Kathryn A. Davis
Prem Phyak

1
INTRODUCTION

The 2014 *Language Policy* thematic issue edited by Davis (Volume 13, Issue 2) introduced *Engaged Language Policy and Practices* (Davis, 2014) as an alternative approach to language policy studies. We draw on this earlier conceptualization toward a more in-depth and nuanced understanding of the political, individual, and ideological nature of engaged language policy-making and practices. We further hold that "it is situated action—collaboratively designing and doing social welfare equity—that brings substantive meaning to our language policy and planning endeavors" (Davis, 2014, p. 83). Thus, this book is designed to address the need for "critically informed and informing transformative dialogue within and across ideological, institutional, and situational spaces" towards realizing equitable policies (Davis, 2014, p. 83). Our engaged language policy and practices (ELP) approach involves documenting the processes involved in advocating for the means by which inequitable policies are created and equitable policies are shaped, planned, and implemented. Central to this approach is engagement of all concerned, such as government officials, educators, community members, and students, in dialogue and action toward equitable language policies and education. Our ELP perspective is further informed by a range of theories that include critical analyses (e.g., Bakhtin, 1981; Bourdieu, 1991; Gramsci, 1971; Habermas, 1981; Harvey, 2005), transformative education (e.g., Freire, 1970; hooks, 1994), engaged anthropology (e.g., Hymes, 1969; Low & Merry, 2010), and engaged ethnographic approaches to language policy and practices (e.g., Canagarajah, 2006; Gegeo & Gegeo, 2013; McCarty, 2011; Tollefson, 2013). These and other theories provide the means by which to deconstruct marginalizing ideologies and promote dialogic actions toward equitable policies and practices.

Politics of Engaged Language Policy and Practices

Language policy scholars, sociolinguists, sociologists of language, and critical ethnographers have long brought into question our professional responsibilities within the political arena. Labov's research and political activism (1972, 1982) identified the need for equitable language policies and practices early on. His expert witness role in the *Martin Luther King Jr. Elementary School v. Ann Arbor Board of Education* led to educational policies that recognized and addressed linguistic variation between Black Vernacular and Standard English. Labov went further by subsequently postulating principles to guide professional involvement in political decision-making. The first principle (Labov, 1982) holds that when a researcher becomes aware of a widespread idea or social practice with important consequences that is invalidated by data, he or she is obligated to bring this error to the attention of the widest possible audience. The second principle posits that an investigator who has obtained linguistic data from members of a speech community has an obligation to use that knowledge for the benefit of the community. Third, the principle of linguistic democracy states that linguists should support the use of a standard dialect or language insofar as it is an instrument of wider communication for the general population but oppose its use as a barrier to social mobility. Fourth, the choice of what language or dialect is to be used in a given domain of a speech community is reserved for members of that community.

Wiley (1996) points out that Labov also implicitly holds that a field dominated by members of one group, who study and prescribe remedies for the "problems" of another, needs to ensure representation from the target group in order to guarantee that its voice and insights are not excluded and that assumptions and perspectives of the dominant group are not imposed on it. These principles additionally align with the sociopolitical framing of language maintenance and shift by Fishman (e.g., 1985, 1987, 1991, 1992) who played a leading role in spotlighting ideologies that led to minoritized language loss while at the same time promoting development of local and heritage languages. We use the term *minoritized language* instead of *minority language* to emphasize that all languages and language varieties are equal but often marginalized while others are privileged. Fishman (1992) suggests the need for developing "ideological clarification" that challenges dominant language ideologies toward creating space for minoritized languages in education and other public spheres. Also at the linguistic political forefront since the early 1980s are Tove Skutnabb-Kangas and Robert Phillipson, who vigorously attacked linguistic imperialism and language genocide while relentlessly advocating for language rights, linguistic self-determination, and multilingualism (e.g., Phillipson, 1992; Skutnabb-Kangas, 1990).

Tollefson (1991) and Wiley (1996, 1999) have further provided analyses of language planning studies ranging on a continuum from the neoclassical approach to the more recent historical-structural approach. According to Tollefson (1991, p.

31), the major differences between these two approaches are that the neoclassical emphasizes individual choices, whereas the historical-structural considers the influence of socio-historical factors on language use. In addition, where the neoclassical approach tends to focus more on the current language situation, the historical-structural approach considers past relationships between groups. While the neoclassical approach often presents its evaluations in ahistorical and amoral terms, the historical-structural approach is concerned with issues of class dominance and oppression. Finally, the neoclassical model typically assumes that the field of applied linguistics and teachers is apolitical while the historical-structural approach concludes that a political stance is inescapable, for those who avoid political questions inadvertently support the status quo.

A historical-structural approach to analyses of language policies and plans was subsequently adopted by scholars such as LoBianco (1999), Moore (1996), Pennycook (1994), Phillipson (1988, 1992), Skutnabb-Kangas (1990), Street (1995), Tollefson (1995) and Wiley (1996, 1999). Wiley specifically pointed out the need for analyses of the political, economic, and ideological motivations behind development of language policies. He further addressed the ways in which, based on sociopolitical and economic motivations, politicians manufacture consent among their constituency (see also Apple, 1989). LoBianco (1999) encapsulated these notions of motivation and the manufacturing of consent through analyses of political discourse in which "the object of language planning's attention is also the means of its making, viz language" (p. 69). For example, LoBianco describes the ways in which English-only discourse in the United States is framed and presented to the general public in terms of advancing the empowerment of linguistic minorities through claiming English language "qualities of opportunity, worldliness and success" as opposed to native language associations with "poverty, isolation and marginality" (p. 69). Recognition of the need for equitable language policy has subsequently promoted analyses of the social, political, and economic motivations behind language policies as well as the political discourses that serve to advance these policies.

Given the applied linguists noted here and many other researchers have made important contributions in the political arena, we call for more in-depth articulation of theories and practices of advocacy concerning the intersecting social, cultural, political, and economic conditions of language use and attitudes. This book further strives to provide critique of both current and alternative research philosophies, methods, and policies that have characterized historically structured language policy studies (e.g., Davis, 1994, 1999; Hornberger, 1988; McCarty, 2011). Engaged language policy and practices (ELP) encompasses concepts portrayed throughout this book. We argue for recognition of and support for both national and local language policies and practices for social equity. ELP further focuses on an engaged approach that promotes involvement of all concerned—parents, students, teachers, and administrators—in local policy-making and support for multilingual practices. We centrally uphold the right and need for community-based policies and practices that attend to the social-emotional language and educational needs of marginalized populations. We further argue that equitable language policy and practices are possible through ideological awareness that strengthens the marginalized and other language policy agents' agency, advocacy, and activism.

The Personal is Political

We acknowledge the means by which taken-for-granted national and transnational policies often negate language and culture identities that the indigenous and diaspora hold dear. Native American author David Treuer, in his novel *Little*, poignantly portrays his personal experience of language and culture loss.

> With my feet in the black dirt I continued my work. I tried to think of my work in our language. Digging, dandelions, worm, gentian. I had forgotten so many words, even though I had been here for only a short time. Still, now, there are words we no longer use, phrases that used to anchor us to our trees and our river that we don't speak anymore. Maybe that's what this is—that words get lonely like people do, get hungry like we hunger. They get jealous, they scheme. Maybe this is the words struggling to break the surface of the rippled long stretch of silence. We all were cut away from our parents, but we were cut loose from our words too…we were cut adrift and unmoored from our beautiful sweet words.
> (Adapted from David Treuer, 1995, p. 59)

Our journey toward realizing engaged policy and practices is embedded in the personal experience named by Treuer's reminder of how loss of words—languages—can engender a devastating loss of personal and communal self. The words, ceremony, and elder wisdom that anchor community in heritage ways of being are often taken away from children through migration and alien forms of schooling. Native American, immigrant, and migrant children are frequently distanced from their parents and set adrift from a sense of belonging through unfamiliar language practices that replace rather than are enriched by multiple intersecting selves. We seek here the means by which to support children's experiential range of emotional and socio-cognitive selves that are too often denied by limiting choice to dominant language monolingualism or restricted multilingualism. We thus draw on our language activist elders in seeking to engage communities, parents, youth, children, and concerned others in claiming the right of linguistic and identity choice. This choice becomes increasingly complex in a neoliberal world that promotes global English language spread and a postmodern world in which nations and individuals become increasingly multilingual and multicultural.

While strengthening language and identity diversity offers potential for developing creative communicative repertoires across age and place, language policies have tended toward neoliberal ideologies. The home languages of those dislocated to safe locations due to war and/or poverty are often threatened by national language policies and cultural practices that are alien to migrant populations. In Europe and other countries where official languages have been firmly established, policy makers and educators may promote official national languages while recognizing the hardship of parents and children in doing so. With an expanding European Community (EC) and long-term refugee migration, the French language and culture, for example, are rigidly enforced in public schools in the face of increasing linguistic, ideological, and identity diversity (Hélot & Ó Laoire, 2011). In Europe and globally, while nations adhere to long-held national policies, immigrant languages are often minoritized. That is, while all languages and language varieties are equal, some languages are marginalized, and others are privileged. Fishman (1992) focuses on the importance of developing "ideological clarification" to challenge dominant language ideologies toward creating space for these minoritized languages in education and other public spheres. While British mainstream schools remain English-dominant, community established "complementary" schools further recognize students' multilingual practices and cultural histories and identities (Blackledge & Creese, 2010). These schools provide an alternative language education model that can help conceptualize politically informed language planning in an era of linguistic diversity (see Chapter 4 for detailed discussion).

In exploring global language ideologies that affect policies and practices, we recognize, theorize, and portray the *politics* and *processes* of language policies as shaped by global sociopolitical and economic ideologies. We further call for on-the-ground language practices that resist, negotiate, and appropriate inequitable policies. Our approach draws teachers, students, parents, communities, university experts/advocates, policy makers, and all concerned others into dialogic exploration of language and education policy as nonlinear processes; covert ideologies and policies as potentially marginalizing; and plurilingual/diversity policies as often desirable, effective, and possible. We further demonstrate how counter-public discourses can challenge dominant neoliberal and other damaging ideologies while supporting practices that meet local language, education, economic, and human welfare needs. This engaged conceptualization also involves attention to interdisciplinarity, fluidity, and multiplicity in which the agency of those most impacted by restrictive policies and plans are at the forefront of our endeavors. We also draw on examples of engaged work worldwide toward conceptualizing ELP. However, given that we are creating engagement in the process of theorizing it, models of engaged processes are just now emerging. Thus, we seek to provide here the basis for further theorizing and describing processes of ELP that take place at national, regional, and local levels.

Language Diversity and Imposed Policies

The small country of Luxembourg in the heart of Europe represents the challenges of balancing superdiversity with national identity through language. Luxembourgish is the official national language while German and French act as official languages for use in schools and courts of law, respectively. While encouraging immigration and border crossing commuting to supplement a much-needed French- and German-speaking labor force for international banking, the country is faced with the challenges of regulating a dramatic increase in language/cultural diversity (Weber, 2014). Although Luxembourgers have historically drawn on multilingualism for both official and social purposes, especially among the middle class and elite (Davis, 1994), current plurilingualism appears to represent a linguistic phenomenon that crosses class, ethnicity, and heritage language backgrounds. The current population of 549,700 speak 174 languages, 68 of which have more than 200 speakers (Horner, 2009). Yet while the majority of native and naturalized citizens embrace a Grand Duchy national identity through use of Luxembourgish, schooling in German and French tends to marginalize students who have home languages other than these two media of instruction.

Nepal, a country in the Himalayas, represents a case of extensive indigenous multilingualism that is being challenged by neoliberal English language ideology. The government has introduced an official "mother-tongue-based multilingual education" policy that aims to promote the use of local languages as mediums of instruction up to Grade 3 (see Ministry of Education, 2010). Yet, most recently, a de facto English-as-the-medium-of-instruction policy has created increased educational, economic, and social welfare inequities between the elite and villagers. Phyak (2016a) suggests that this English language policy has been shaped by two major ideologies—*English as a global language* and *English as social capital*—that ignore the local multilingual and multicultural realities surrounding students' everyday lives. The policy further disregards evidence that students' home languages can be a resource for learning both content and language.

Language and cultural diversity in the United States have been significantly challenged during the last 10 years through the *No Child Left Behind* initiative and currently with the *Common Core Standards* mandate. Nationwide suppression of multilingualism through promotion of English and use of standardized testing in public schools has resulted in a significant increase in dropout rates, especially among the poor and immigrant populations. Hawai'i represents a range of challenges to equitable education as diversity increases. The US 2000 Census *Demographic Profile of Foreign-Language Speakers* for Hawai'i indicates that of 1.4 million residents, more than 360,000 are speakers of languages other than English and more than 88,000 are from non-English-language-speaking households (not including the Hawai'i Creole English-speaking majority). According to the 2010

US Census, the percentage of Pacific Islanders who have moved to Hawai'i has increased by 26 percent in the last 10 years and is rising.

A steady stream of migrants from both the Philippines and Pacific Islands continues to arrive in search of work, health care and, increasingly, through dislocation due to global warming. Burkett (2011) details the challenges of increased global warming migration. She states:

> As the effects of climate change intensify, time is running out for millions living in Asia Pacific coastal and island communities. Many will be forced to leave their homes within the next half-century because of increased intensity and frequency of storms and floods, sea-level rise, and desertification. The low lying small island states of the Pacific are especially endangered; residents there may lose not only their homes, but their entire nations.
>
> (p. 1)

As dislocation and relocation intensify, a crisis of language and social diversity is emerging. While all social services are impacted by increasing migration to the state, adequate and equitable language education is a priority need. Not only are much-needed Pacific Islander languages being lost through English-only education, but nearly 50 percent of this student population is dropping out of school. The Hawai'i Department of Education and University of Hawai'i College of Education have so far failed to provide policies and plans that offer comprehensive and effective language minoritized education. The college has never had either an English language learner (ELL) or bilingual/multilingual teacher education program. Instead, the Department of Education has relied on workshops to train teachers, currently in "scientifically based" ELL strategies promoted by the for-profit World-class Instructional Design and Assessment Corporation. Immigrant children and youth clearly require quality bilingual/multilingual schooling for educational success through college. At the same time, these students potentially offer valuable future resources through providing for much-needed interpretation and translation skills across professional and social services. The recent Federal *Every Child Achieves Act of 2015 Title I* allows states to develop their own accountability systems. The bill thus ends absolute federal control by restoring to states the responsibility for determining how to use the federally required tests for accountability purposes. The bill specifically indicates the following:

> States must include these (federal) tests in their accountability systems, but will be able to determine the weight of those tests in their systems. States will also be required to include graduation rates, one measure of postsecondary education or workforce readiness, and English proficiency

for English learners. States will also be permitted to include other measures of student and school performance in their accountability systems in order to provide teachers, parents, and other stakeholders with a more accurate determination of school performance.

(p.1)

It remains to be seen how this new bill impacts state policy as well as those who have been most marginalized by federal policies, in effect teachers and students.

In moving beyond Nepal, Hawai'i, and Luxembourg, we note the increasing migration of refugees escaping from ISIS war and terror that have escalated in 2015 and are progressively challenging the resources of stable nation-states worldwide (FactCheck.Org, 2015). The United Nations High Commissioner for Refugees—which refers to refugees for resettlement in other countries—states that there are currently more than 4 million registered Syrian refugees. Figures on the demographic makeup of refugees indicate that 2.1 million were registered by the United Nations High Commissioner for Refugees in Egypt, Iraq, Jordan, and Lebanon. Another 1.9 million Syrian refugees have been registered by the government of Turkey and more than 24,000 were registered in North Africa (PBS, 2013). The International Organization for Migration estimates that more than 464,000 migrants have further entered Europe by crossing the Mediterranean Sea in the first 9 months of 2015. Syrians fleeing their country's four-and-a-half-year-old civil war made up the largest group (39 percent). Afghans escaping the ongoing war with Taliban rebels (11 percent), and Eritreans fleeing forced labor (7 percent) made up the second- and third-largest groups of migrants. Deteriorating security and crushing poverty in Iraq, Nigeria, Pakistan, Somalia, and Sudan have also contributed to the migrant influx. While Europe takes the brunt of migration, Canada and the United States have agreed to take in a limited number of refugees. As the ongoing and so far unresolved migratory crisis continues, eventual relocation will call on a range of services to meet refugee needs. From the perspective of language policy and practices, both adults and children will need support in learning the language and culture of their host country. One refugee stated in a German *Der Spiegel* newspaper interview, "I came here because Germany is safe; there is no war. Germany is the best in Europe. France is no good, you cannot get language classes there, but in Germany you can learn the language for free." Further language issues are likely to arise through the immediate need for interpretation and translation and likely long-term schooling issues regarding formulation of equitable education programs for refugee/migrant children. The November 13, 2015 brutal terrorist attacks in Paris and Brussels have prompted conditions of transnational war and the need for compassionate communication among those who escape as opposed to those who participate in the dark ISIS movement.

Policy Advocacy

In the face of local, nation-state, and global crises and struggles such as those described above, Tollefson (2013) suggests the need for drawing on notions of public sphere and "subaltern counterpublics" as they operate in maintaining the status quo or work toward formation of equitable language and other policies and practices. He states,

> While a dominant public sphere is often maintained by state authorities, large national media, and other powerful forces, there are also many smaller public spheres, some of which (e.g., the African-American press in the United States) help form "subaltern counterpublics" that provide counter-hegemonic discourses challenging the discourse of the dominant public sphere (Gegeo & Watson-Gegeo, 2002). Many researchers working within this paradigm offer an optimistic vision of the potential for creating actions within communities, in a metaphorical space of discussion, negotiation, and compromise that can be sustained despite coercive, top-down language policies, in part through modern communications media that have expanded the range of the public sphere.
>
> (p. 28)

We find the "subaltern counterpublics" approach essential in framing efforts of resistance and change toward recognition of the multiple, fluid, creative, and localized ways in which communication is or can be realized. While nation-states fear that multilingualism will threaten national cohesion, there is evidence of increased diversity of language and ideologies that can be used to promote equitable policies and practices (Skutnabb-Kangas & Heugh, 2012). These include challenges to pervasive neoliberalism; recognition of inclusive multilingualism such as demonstrated in hip-hop, street vernaculars, and language varieties; and possible privileging of localized policies over elite and/or nationally controlled education. While US rappers initiated this identity form, global musicians now localize hip-hop to give voice to their own styles, language repertoires, and political stances. Pennycook reports on global hip-hop including a pan-Pacific hip-hop network among Samoan, Hawaiian, Māori, and other Pacific Islanders (Pennycook, 2007). He identifies *Sudden Rush* as having developed "ne mele paleoleo, Hawaiian hip-hop, a cut n' mix of African and Jamaican reggae rhythms, Hawaiian chanting and subversive rapping in the Hawaiian language" (Akindes, 2001, p. 91). Pennycook further documents the French hip-hop scenes in Paris and Marseille in France; Dkar, Abidjan, and Libreville in West Africa; and Montreal in Quebec (Alim, Ibrahim, & Pennycook, 2009; Pennycook, 2013).

Coupland (2007, p. 3) points to the importance of understanding "how people use or enact or perform social styles for a range of symbolic purposes."

Eckert (2004, p. 43) observes that this enables us to see that "style (like language) is not a thing but a practice." In reflecting back on Treuer's (1995) observation that "words struggle to break the surface of the rippled long stretch of calm," we suggest that youth also claim and recreate their "beautiful, sweet, tricky words" in the style of hip-hop, street vernacular and translanguaging (García & Li, 2014). Otheguy, García, and Reid (2015) define translanguaging as "the deployment of a speaker's full linguistic repertoire without regard for watchful adherence to the socially and politically defined boundaries of named (and usually national and state) languages" (p. 283). Acknowledging youth's complete linguistic repertoires, including localized and transnational language trends, suggests further avenues of inclusion toward arresting the tide of marginalizing discourses in schools and elsewhere. Globalization, cultural flows, and subversive messages that counter nation-state ideals represent diversity phenomena that are being played out through localized movements. For example, as previously mentioned, "complementary" schools support home language use toward acknowledging multilingualism (Blackledge & Creese, 2010). Davis et al. (2005) specifically argue for schooling that promotes success among marginalized student populations when, rather than standardized curriculum and tests, diverse populations of students are at the center of their own learning. Thus, in acknowledging the richness and diversity of youth identities and languages, students can develop a flexible language and identity repertoire that more comfortably aligns with postmodern complexity and fluidity (see Chapter 4 for a more detailed description of language practices).

The Political is Personal

Post-modern and sociopolitical shifts have prompted language researchers to explore policies as shaped by global sociopolitical and economic ideologies while calling for on-the-ground language studies and practices that resist, negotiate, and appropriate inequitable policies (Davis, 2009b, 2014; Johnson, 2013; Wyman, McCarty, & Nicholas, 2014). We further argue for an ELP approach that draws language policy agents into critical dialogue toward identifying, challenging, and transforming hegemonic language ideologies that inform dominant language policies and practices (Davis, 2014; Phyak & Bui, 2014). We also promote counter-public discourses that challenge dominant neoliberal ideologies that threaten the identities, languages, and epistemologies of indigenous and other marginalized populations. In upholding the right to multilingual practices in schools and other public and private spheres (Gegeo & Watson-Gegeo, 2001; Tollefson, 2013), ELP seeks to support local participants in meeting their language, education, economic, and human welfare needs. Thus, ELP conceptualization involves attention to interdisciplinarity, fluidity, and multiplicity in which the agency of individuals and communities is considered the epicenter of language policy reform (Davis, 2014; Menken & García, 2010). This is especially important in an era of xenophobia that threatens language and social intolerance of those associated with but not guilty of terrorism.

In re-envisioning language policy and planning as an engaged approach, we draw on and portray theoretical and educational equity perspectives through global and local dialogic efforts. We discuss ways in which communities are engaged in agentive processes toward transforming marginalizing educational and social welfare policies. Thus, we offer an alternative to traditional top-down language education policy-making through depicting how ELP embodies the intersection of *political* and *personal* critical inquiry; ongoing engaged language planning *processes* with full participant involvement; and *portrayal* of ongoing outcomes. This approach to policy activism further suggests alternative research conceptualization and documentation.

Scholars concerned with equity issues from a range of fields and disciplines have for some time considered the complex ideological nature of stated and implied language education policies and practices (Piller, 2016; Tollefson, 2013). Specialists suggest that policies are commonly guided by ideologies such as standardization, modernization, neoliberalism, and "so-called" equity of opportunity while ignoring local diversity needs and resources (García, 2009; May, 2014). In addressing these issues, we take an ELP approach to language education policy-making that draws communities of teachers, students, parents, and communities into dialogic exploration of ineffective and marginalizing language policies and practices. This approach promotes counter-public discourses that challenge dominant neoliberal ideologies while supporting policies and practices that meet local language, education, economic, and human welfare needs. Engaged processes effectively suggest local determination of schooling that recognizes language/identity fluidity and multiplicity while upholding the agency of all participants. Toward these ends, this book explores a range of issues relevant to addressing language and social equity issues.

Organization of the Book

This book is organized into six chapters. While Chapter 1 provides an introduction to the book, Chapter 2 forefronts the exploration of language ideologies shaping public discourses concerning language policies and practices. This chapter further suggests the essential and central position of ideological analyses in work with parents, educators, community members, students, and others toward raising awareness of the underlying tenets of operating systems such as neoliberal commodification, standardized language education policies, English language spread, and how these impact the education of linguistically, culturally, and socioeconomically diverse student populations. We further explore the meanings of global and situated (local) ideologies in terms of how these intersect and diverge toward either productive or restrictive education.

In Chapter 3, we explore engaged ethnography as a method for bringing about transformative language policy processes. Engaged ethnography frames and portrays our overall approach as political in nuanced and public ways toward promoting the means by which the dispossessed work to possess the right to research, advocate, and acquire sustainable, equitable, and self-defined honorable ways of learning and living. Like other critical research approaches (Cammarota & Fine, 2008; Fine, 2006; Freire, 1970), engaged ethnography of language policies and practices works toward placing participants at the center of investigations while striving to awaken a sense of injustice among those with material and cultural power. Yet ELP further aims to describe and portray ways in which all concerned individuals and institutions—policymakers, administrators, teachers, parents/community members, students, schools, local organizations—are joined in processes of developing awareness of inequitable ideologies as well as the means by which to challenge inhumane, demeaning, and exclusionary policies and practices from within.

Chapter 4 on planning resistance and discovering alternative ideologies and policies suggests that once marginalizing and ineffective national, state, and regional language ideologies and policies are uncovered, they require addressing through exploration of effective, equitable, and theoretically informed resistance. We draw here on ideological analyses as well as deep understandings of *what is* and *what should be* to inform movement toward *what can be*. We specifically explore and describe ways in which ELP works as an all-inclusive community of forward-looking participants dedicated to innovative and collective exploration of policies, plans, and practices that best serve their children. Following this, we discuss development of relevant and engaging policies and practices that emphasize the need for supporting teachers and building on local knowledge toward schooling that is relevant and engaging. Thus, we reveal and model engaged practices that reflect current theories and practices toward addressing linguistic and educational inequality. These practices reflect an increasing sense of an interactive local and global identity that rejects neoliberalism, embraces diversity, and resists inequitable policies and practices through taking up post-structuralist language and identity perspectives.

Chapter 5 explores development of relevant and engaging policies and practices through emphasizing the need for supporting teachers and building on local knowledge toward schooling that is relevant and engaging. Thus, we reveal and model engaged practices that draw on current theories and practices toward addressing linguistic and educational inequality. These practices reflect an increasing sense of an interactive local and global identity that rejects neoliberalism, embraces diversity, and resists inequitable policies and practices through taking up post-structuralist language and identity perspectives.

Concluding Chapter 6 summarizes the intersection of theories and methods toward informing language policies and practices. We more specifically explore language policy issues that recur across geographic contexts worldwide and either reflect inequality or represent progress toward ideological awareness and social transformation. We further describe the means by which a cross-section of inquiry approaches that include Freire's pedagogy of the oppressed, participatory action research and engaged ethnography inform transformative language policy processes. Thus, we explore the means by which to contest inequitable language policies and build ideological awareness toward equitable education and socioeconomic well-being.

2
LANGUAGE POLICIES AND IDEOLOGICAL ANALYSES

Pierre Bourdieu was among the first to suggest in his landmark book *Distinction: A Social Critique of the Judgment of Taste* (1984) that language policy and use are ideologically driven. He argues that legitimization of particular languages and dialects in education and other public spheres are determined by sociopolitical and economic power relations. In other words, the choice of language(s) and language varieties for education, mass media, government administration, and the economic market is not a neutral and objective determination but rather an ideological process that encompasses historical, political, and economic power relations. Blommaert (2013), McCarty, Collins, and Hopson (2011), and Pennycook (2013) have subsequently argued for historical and sociopolitical awareness of language ideologies and their role in supporting or delegitimizing languages/dialects and those who use them. In this chapter, we first discuss the historical construction of ideologies and then analyze how the specific dominant ideologies of standard language, linguistic nationalism, and commodification marginalize minoritized languages, their speakers, and nonstandard language practices. We then describe the processes and intended outcomes of engaged ideological analysis.

The Historical Construction of Language Ideology

Gramsci (1971) was the first to go beyond Marx's material interpretation of inequality in production, distribution, and consumption of resources by alternatively suggesting control through "soft power" over subalterns. Gramsci more specifically suggests that hegemony occurs as an "organizing principle" as beliefs, ideas, and worldviews of one class dominate another. Hegemony as domination through consent occurs when individuals or groups unquestionably embrace social hierarchy as the natural condition. Gramsci's theory of hegemony thus offers a framework for understanding how the general public buys into dominant language ideologies, such as "one nation, one language" (Fishman, 1980) and more recent propaganda concerning the superiority of English in elite standard forms (Block, Gray, & Holborow, 2012; Holborow, 2015; Ricento, 2015).

Purcell (2002, 2009) provides an accessible description of neoliberal meanings represented as a complex mixture of laissez- and aidez-faire policies. He suggests that while the state increases support for capital, it retrenches assistance for citizens, especially the poor and vulnerable. He suggests that "… direct aid to families, unemployment insurance, social security, public housing, child care, and health care have been reduced, offloaded onto local governments or eliminated altogether" (Purcell, 2009). Harvey (2005) further acknowledged that retrenched social policy produces an increasing population of marginalized and desperate people. A common state strategy for addressing this social condition has been disciplinary: zero tolerance policies, workfare controls, punitive policing, and expanded imprisonment (e.g., Davis, 1990). Althusser (1971) further developed a theory of "Ideological States Apparatuses (ISAs)" to describe how state mechanisms such as school and church govern people ideologically rather than "by violence" and "repressive forces." A case in point is the creation and maintenance of "No Child Left Behind" federal legislation that subsequently marginalized immigrants, migrants, and the poor through state-supported curriculum and regulatory standardized testing that advantaged *those who have* (middle-/upper-class families who speak English and are familiar with mainstream school ideology) and *those who have not* (immigrants/migrants/the poor) who speak other/nonstandard languages and have restricted access to acquiring language and school knowledge.

Experiences of being marginalized and discriminated against emerge from sociopolitical inequalities. Thus, engaging in humanitarian language education welfare then specifically involves identification and critique of marginalizing ideologies that are reproduced in dominant language policies and practices. Analysis involves empowerment of the disenfranchised toward denaturalizing and then transforming harmful ideologies. This necessitates engaging participants in critical analysis of both public sphere (Habermas, 1989) and counter-public sphere ideologies (Fraser, 1990; Warner, 2002). Critical neo-Marxist theorist, Jürgen Habermas (1989), specifically argues that public sphere ideologies are reproduced by communicative actions that he defines as reification of consciousness through differentiated symbolic structures (i.e., economic and structural power relations). Habermas (1985) further contends that the elites who have control over economic resources and state mechanisms (e.g., bureaucracy) largely dominate communicative actions and "condition the responses of those subordinate to him [sic], … without having to depend primarily on their willingness to cooperate" (p. 268). Therefore, public sphere ideologies serve the interests of those who have control over the production, circulation, and use or consumption of legitimate language resources through mass media, education, and other state and non-state apparatus. While public sphere ideologies are constructed through "authoritative discourses" such as state policies, counter-public sphere ideologies represent "internally persuasive discourses" toward countering harmful dominant discourses (Bakhtin, 1981). The authoritative discourses support standard language and monolingual ideologies that are unquestionably taken for granted and provide no room for alternative discourses. On the other hand, internally persuasive discourses, which emerge from people's struggles and tensions with dominant discourses, embrace grassroots language practices and ideologies.

The construction of public and counter-public spheres in language policy depends on the question of who determines language policies; whose voices are heard; whose identities and interests are represented; what counts as language and whose languages count; and who benefits from or is marginalized by particular language policies and practices. While providing a critical analysis of linguistic inequalities emanating from current neoliberal justification of English as a global language, Tollefson (2013) argues that it is necessary for language policy scholars to construct counter-public language ideologies and practices toward recognizing minoritized languages and language practices as resources for education and other purposes. To this end, it is essential that scholars and educational practitioners explore local/global ideologies and their impact on the lived experience of the disenfranchised and include this analysis in the policy-making process.

Important considerations in conducting ideological analysis include identification of marginalizing ideologies; analysis of the intersection of these ideologies with sociopolitical and economic conditions; and empowerment of participants to transform hegemonic ideologies into situated and trans-/national achievement of equitable language policies and practices. All of these considerations are present in ongoing struggles within contact zones of contradictory ideologies toward "ideological becoming" intended to promote awareness that leads to activism and language policy transformation. Engaged ideological analysis first looks closely at how language policies and practices are linked with the historicity of political and economic conditions (Davis, 2014). This analysis does not simply report ideologies observed by researchers but instead engages all concerned in critical dialogue toward raising awareness of linguistic inequalities and injustice. Engaging in ideological analysis allows subalterns to identify their exclusion from language policy-making while seeking the means by which to take control over this process. Thus, through gaining ideological awareness of sociopolitical inequalities, subalterns can recognize inequitable language policies and, consequently, promote equitable policies and practices at local and national levels.

Language Ideologies and Multilingualism

Europe in the twenty-first century has been characterized by what is known as super-diversity (Vertovec, 2007). Current linguistic landscape complexity is the result of unprecedented movement of people, finance, technology, ideas, and knowledge (Appadurai, 1996). Blommaert and Rampton (2011) suggest that super-diversity is characterized by complexity and fluid hybrid multilingual/multicultural practices. Yet, despite the tremendous increase in diversity, education policy makers have largely failed to recognize the resources and challenges of new multilingual student populations (Conteh & Meier, 2014; Skutnabb-Kangas & Heugh, 2012). May (2014) argues that traditional language ideologies that assume monolingualism (and in some cases bilingualism) as the norm are still dominant in educational policies and applied linguistic research. Blommaert (1999, 2008) and Benson (2014), among others, suggest the need to explore nation-state histories of language ideologies toward understanding and counteracting monolingual education for multilingual populations.

Silverstein (1979) was among the first to define language ideologies, also known as linguistic ideology and ideology of language, as "sets of beliefs about language articulated by users as a rationalization or justification of perceived language structure and use" (p. 193). As previously mentioned, beliefs about "correct" or "acceptable" languages for institutional or other uses are deeply rooted in cultural, sociopolitical, and economic histories of peoples and nations (Blommaert, 1999; Gal, 2005; Jaffe, 2009; Pietikäinen & Kelly-Holmes, 2013). Makihara and Schieffelin (2007) consider language ideology as "cultural representations, whether explicit or implicit, of the intersection of language and human beings in a social world" (p. 14). They argue that ideologies link language to identity, power, aesthetics, morality, and epistemology. These links then "underpin not only linguistic form and use, but also significant social institutions and fundamental notions of persons and community" (p. 14). In this way, language ideologies constitute sociopolitical power relations and people's consciousness about their own identities, conditions of oppression/marginalization, and access to sociopolitical resources. While Kroskrity (2009) claims that language ideologies often "represent the perception of language and discourse that is constructed in the interest of a specific social or cultural group" (pp. 72–73), these ideologies also encompass sociopolitical and economic positions that are articulated through implicit and explicit language policy and practices.

At the more implicit level, language ideologies constitute degrees of awareness, positionality, and self-interest as enacted in the process of policy-making. Thus, engaging in language ideological analysis demands critical investigation of sociopolitical inequalities, historical oppression, and linguistic discrimination emanating from governmental and economic self-interest (Blommaert, 1999; Blommaert & Verschueren, 1998; Gal, 2005; Irvine, 1989; Jaffe, 1999; Kroskrity,

2004; Weber, 2009). Linguistic anthropologists Susan Gal (1989), Judith Irvine (1989), and Paul Friedrich (1989) were among the first to consider language ideologies as part of the political and economic condition. These scholars argue that the hegemony of monolingual ideology demands standardization in school and the mass media and, thus, is constitutive of inequitable political and economic power for speakers of other languages.

In considering language ideology an historical object, Blommaert (1999, 2006) traces the particular histories of creation and enforcement of language policies. For example, the ideological construction of language as a homogenous entity and symbol of national identity, which Anderson (1991) calls an "imagined community," is historically rooted in eighteenth- and nineteenth-century discourse concerning the creation of the nation-state. During British and French nationalist movements, only Standard English and French, respectively, were considered legitimate languages of national identity. Other languages as well as nonstandard dialects of both English and French are not commonly recognized as legitimate modes of official communication. This standard language ideology, which Milroy (2001, p. 1) defines as "the belief that there is one and only one correct spoken form of the language, modeled on a single correct written form…is drawn primarily from the language of the upper middle class" (Lippi-Green, 1997, p. 64). Thus, a standard language ideology privileged through the sociopolitical power of the upper-/middle-class marginalizes the lower class by failing to recognize their language practices within public spheres such as education and other official state apparatus (also Lippi-Green, 2000).

In their critical historiography of language ideologies, Makoni and Pennycook (2005, 2007) also support the view that construction of language as a fixed and homogenous object was "invented" as part of seventeenth- and eighteenth-century Christian/colonial and nationalist intent. For these scholars, the essentialized monolingual ideology as part of Western European "governmentality" (Foucault, 1991) intentionally fails to represent *reallinguistik* practices characterized by fluidity, multiplicity, and plurilingualism. Thus, they argue that it would be necessary to "disinvent" the monolingual ideology of language in order to create language policies that promote true multilingualism. The disinvention process includes alternative ways of reimagining language from the perspective of embracing actual language practices at local levels. For this to occur, critical examination is needed of ideologies represented in current language policies and practices. As Makoni and Pennycook (2005) argue, an additive approach to bilingual education policies may reproduce rather than challenge an ideology of official language as a fixed, enumerative, and monolingual entity. García (2009) and Flores and Rosa (2015) also contend that additive bilingualism may reproduce the same monolingual ideology that considers native speaker proficiency, rather than multilingual development, as the model for assessment. These scholars argue that the additive approach to bilingual education reproduces standard language ideology that discriminates against minoritized language speakers.

The colonial invention of language as a bounded object has further been institutionally reproduced in language policies within the postcolonial context. In analyzing findings from linguistic survey studies in Africa and India, Makoni and Pennycook (2005) found that European linguists invented languages through practicing their own ideology of standardization to govern people who speak diverse languages. Through various projects such as dictionary creation, linguistic survey, language mapping, and script development, European linguists systematically imposed homogeneity and ignored the local linguistic diversity and identity of minoritized language speakers. This "Western language ideology" (Dorian, 1998) created three central premises in language policy discourse: bilingualism is onerous and subordinated; nonstandardized languages are contemptible; and social Darwinism of language as linguistic "survival of the fittest" is justified (Dorian, 1998, p. 10; also see Farr & Song, 2011; King, 2000). Despite the continual efforts of communities to promote multilingualism at the local level around the world, Western monolingual language ideologies are deeply entrenched, leading to blinding teachers, parents, policy makers, and the general public to the benefits of multilingualism.

Through analyses of ideologies of language policies and practices in the US, Farr and Song (2011) reveal how the standard English-only policy for schooling was rooted in fear of mass European migration during the early twentieth century and German influence arising from two world wars. Thus, an ideology of English serves as the legitimate marker of American national identity. Despite being a multilingual country, Farr and Song (2011) argue that the US educational policies and practices continue to reproduce a monolingual model and standard language ideology in schools. A number of studies have shown that the imposition of standard language practices negatively affects the educational achievement of minoritized children (Cummins, 2006; Farr & Song, 2011; Skutnabb-Kangas & Heugh, 2012). Farr and Song (2011) further argue that the standard English language ideology not only deprives multilingual students of learning opportunities but it furthers an "ideology of contempt" (Dorian, 1998) toward subordinate languages and dialects and their speakers.

Tsui and Tollefson (2007) are critical of a standard language ideology that fails to recognize the language practices of multilingual speakers as well as accented varieties of English such as Indian English, Jamaican English and African American English. As nonstandard languages are labeled linguistically deficient, policies that promote standard language ideology create a hierarchy among languages and their speakers. Despite these consequences, Ricento (2006) argues that Western-based ideologies are systematically reproduced in language policies with the belief that "monolingualism is necessary for social and economic equality" (p. 14). Yet studies from postcolonial contexts such as the

Philippines (e.g., Tupas, 2015) and India (Annamalai, 2013; Ramanathan, 2006) further reveal the means by which Western language ideologies intentionally create inequitable hierarchies and, subsequently, realize ideological and implementational challenges in promoting multilingual education within and across national boundaries. Canagarajah and Ashraf (2013) further argue that India's trilingual policy (Hindi, English, and a local/indigenous language) is shaped by a monolingual ideology that defines language as a bounded object. They hold that such policies are not sufficient for addressing multilingual practices, which are characterized by fluidity and simultaneity of languages.

Given that a mother-tongue ideology links language with ethnicity and race, policies based on the bounded language ideology often fail to embrace increasing linguistic diversity and complex language practices (Gupta, 1997; Khubchandani, 2003). Moreover, the dominant early-exit language transitional language education model in the United States and elsewhere fails to promote multilingual literacies and effective education in the long run (Baker, 2011; Ball, 2010). To address multilingualism, children are often taught in their home languages during the early grades but then switch to the national or dominant language in the higher grades. For example, the current "mother tongue–based multilingual education policy" of Nepal states that indigenous children are to be taught in their "mother tongue" up to Grade 3 and, in Nepali, from Grade 4 onward (Ministry of Education, 2010; Phyak, 2013).

Erasure of Multilingual Practices

The reproduction of Western ideologies in national language policies and practices systematically contributes to the erasure of minoritized languages and multilingual practices. Erasure that "renders some persons or activities or sociolinguistic phenomena invisible" occurs when "facts that are inconsistent with the ideological scheme either go unnoticed or get explained away" (Irvine & Gal, 2000, p. 38). Irvine and Gal further suggest that fractal recursivity—or a repeating pattern of monolingual policy and usage—eventually leads to the erasure of the fluid and heteroglossic language practices of multilingual children. Studies show that the erasure of students' home language practices from school not only creates learning challenges for multilingual children but diminishes their voices, identities, and literacy practices (Conteh & Meier, 2014; García, 2009).

A growing number of studies from around the world shows that allowing students' home languages in the classroom enhances learning of language and academic skills (Baker, 2011; Thomas & Collier, 2000). Cummins (2006) argues that the use of students' home languages and bi-/multilingual practices in school is indispensable in empowering students and ensuring their engagement in deeper cognitive understandings and investment in learning. In "imagining multilingual schools," García, Skutnabb-Kangas, and Torres-Guzmán

(2006) argue that multilingual language practices are important resources for minimizing the current educational achievement gap between minoritized and dominant language speakers. For these scholars, educational policies must challenge the "monolingual mindset" and embrace "the diversity of language and literacy practices that children and youth bring to school" (p. 14). García et al. (2006) further argue that allowing students' hybrid multilingual practices in school, which Gutiérrez, Baquedano-López, and Álvarez (2001) define as "a systematic, strategic, affiliative, and sense-making process…" (p. 128), provides them with space for learning multilingual literacies, achieving identity investment, and developing critical awareness.

Blackledge and Creese (2014) further deconstruct an ideology of language as a bounded entity and take heteroglossic language practices as pedagogical tools for educating children in multilingual classrooms. Building on Bakhtin's (1981) heteroglossia—hybrid language practices that embrace multivoicedness and multiple discourses—Blackledge and Creese (2014) go beyond a monoglot view of language as a bounded and standard object and suggest that we need to embrace multilingual language practices through which children display multiple voices, identities, cultures, locations, knowledge, and histories. Weber (2014) suggests that a rigid and fixed notion of language in developing policies fails to embrace multilingual practices in school. He holds that it is necessary to adopt a "flexible multilingual policy" to reimagine education from a social equity perspective in globalized and super-diverse world contexts. The ideology of flexibility denounces rigid and imposed language policies that uphold linguistic nationalism and standard language ideologies and rather focuses on children's complete linguistic repertoire as resources for language and academic content learning.

Although there is increased worldwide awareness of the importance of multilingualism, dominant language policies and practices are still reproduced through monolingual, monoglossic and standard language ideologies. Rather than transforming discriminatory ideologies, language policies and practices most often appropriate them (Flores & Rosa, 2015). The erasure of multilingual practices continues to dominate language education through faulty ideologies such as linguistic hierarchies, monoglossic assumptions, and standardized language education. Yet children can greatly benefit from schools that provide safe spaces for using their home language and literacy practices and, thus, move toward more successful learning (Conteh & Meier, 2014; Hajek & Slaughter, 2015). The engaged language policies and practices that we promote here focus on adopting ideologies that are founded on the educational, social, economic, and political best interests of marginalized groups. Before discussing ways in which to engage participants in ideological analyses toward raising critical awareness, we explore how the current political economic ideology— neoliberalism (economic globalization)—is contributing to creating language hierarchies and inequalities.

Commodification of Language and the New Political Economy

We are currently experiencing tremendous social change in the world's political-economic condition in the age of late capitalism (Harvey, 2005). Nation-states and their elected officials increasingly transfer governance to private agencies, multi-national corporations, international financial institutions, and nongovernment organizations to presumably provide effective public services. Yet this shift has created severe difficulties for disenfranchised populations worldwide. The recent financial crisis in Greece and the growing number of Syrian refugees fleeing to Europe represent complex social, political, and economic challenges. While so-called free and competitive market economies result in state deregulation and increased privatization (Harvey, 2005; Lipman, 2011), this new political economic condition, known as *neoliberalism*, has influenced transnational views about what counts as equitable social welfare and productivity in policy and practice. Harvey (2005) defines neoliberalism as:

> [...]a theory of political economic practices that proposes human well-being can best be advanced by liberating individual entrepreneurial freedoms and skills within an institutional framework characterized by strong private property rights, free markets and free trade. The role of the state is to create and preserve an institutional framework appropriate to such practices. The state has to guarantee, for example, the quality and integrity of money. It must also set up those military, defense, police and legal structures and functions required to secure private property rights and to guarantee, by force if need be, the proper functioning of markets.
>
> (p. 2)

He goes on to say that

> [S]tate interventions in markets (once created) must be kept to a bare minimum because, according to the theory, the state cannot possibly possess enough information to second-guess market signals (prices) and because powerful interest groups will inevitably distort and bias state interventions (particularly in democracies) for their own benefit.
>
> (p. 2)

Under the larger discourse of globalization and neoliberalism, "market globalism" (Steger, Goodman, & Wilson, 2012) was first conceived of by Prime Minister Margaret Thatcher in Britain and President Ronald Reagan in the United States as a way to reform economic policies in the early 1980s. The US and UK governments, in the guise of addressing economic crises, intervened and dismantled Keynesian social welfare policies and created new policy arrangements that attacked labor movements and the key principles of social welfare. The resulting deregulated economy granted more power to corporations and private entities. Governments of both countries have subsequently promoted a free flow of money through multinational companies, financial institutions, and corporate houses. The World Bank and the International Monetary Fund are two major entities that draw on the Euro-American capitalist ideology in implementing this worldwide neoliberal political project. As Harvey (2005) argues, neoliberalism "as a mode of discourse" has greatly shaped social policies on a global scale through structural reform projects. As organizing principles for national policies and conditions for receiving grants and loans, these institutions ask nation-states to adopt measures such as deregulation, privatization, massive corporate tax cuts, free markets, global trade, labor wage reduction, and withdrawal of the state from public services.

Neoliberalism subsequently reflects "a new social imaginary" (Lipman, 2011) of the world we currently live in through changed social relations and cultural identities. As the market place rather than the nation-state becomes the most influential means for addressing social issues, human consciousness and behaviors are shaped "…not by collective institutions and interaction, but by supply and demand, by entrepreneurs and consumer choice, by individual companies and individual people" (Holborow, 2015, p. 34). Accordingly, language policies and practices, implicitly and explicitly, embrace the legitimacy of those languages that dominate the local and global marketplace. As education is redefined as a means to produce "human capital" to fill market demand, educational institutions have come to focus on dominant languages and ways of learning such as English and use of standardized curricula and tests. As Bourdieu (1991) argued, the symbolic capital of languages is most often determined by economic capital value of language and language practices in the educational and linguistic marketplace. In other words, the symbolic dominance of language used by the upper social class is subsequently considered a natural condition of society.

Holborow (2015) claims that the legitimization of particular language(s) as a medium of instruction and corresponding elite control over economic capital reproduce linguistic, political, and economic inequalities (also see Block, Gray, & Holborow, 2012). Phillipson (2008) critically examines the global spread of English as an integral part of Anglo-American political and economic interests. He argues that the projection of English as "symbolic capital" in the global linguistic and educational marketplace is indeed a deliberate effort to maintain American and British dominance created through a history of colonization, militarization (toward world rule), and economic accumulation (see Smith, 2003). Phillipson's (2008) critique of neoliberalism further reveals English-as-a-global language as inspired by two implicit ideologies—linguistic nationalism and language-as-commodity. The linguistic nationalism ideology is linked with an Anglo-American desire to develop an imagined global community that speaks the same language, preferably English. In other words, the same language ideology that the United States and the United Kingdom have created intends to unite people under one national identity through promoting English as the lingua franca on a global scale—the phenomenon that Irvine and Gal (2000) call "fractal recursivity."

This Anglo-European ideology, however, does not only apply to English language policies; rather, it is reproduced in other national language policies worldwide. For example, influenced by the British and subsequent India ideology of linguistic nationalism during the colonial period, Nepal adopted a monolingual Nepali-only policy (Awasthi, 2008). Consequently, languages other than Nepali were legally banned in schools and other public spheres up until the early 1990s (Phyak, 2013; Weinberg, 2013). This monolingual ideology is still dominant throughout the country, although some space for minoritized languages is now provided in education and the mass media.

Heller (2010) argues that the dominant nation-state ideology that advocates cultural and political recognition is now re-legitimated and preserved in new ways in late capitalism. The ideology of language as a marker of national identity has gradually been replaced or coupled with the view of language as commodity (i.e.. the assumption that the symbolic value of language is determined by its exchange value on the free market). The ideology of language as commodity thus helps to "explain why certain linguistic forms and practices play the role they do in the production and reproduction of the social order and of the moral order that legitimates it" (Heller, 2010, p. 102). As Bourdieu (1991) claimed, this ideology upholds the assumption that the legitimacy of a particular language in the public sphere is determined exclusively by the material value it is given in the free marketplace. In other words, the languages and linguistic practices recognized as legitimate are those that dominate production, distribution, and consumption of social commodities.

In arguing that commodification of English as a global language is not just a product but also a process and a project, Phillipson (1992, 2008, 2012) acknowledges the linguistic impact of British and American corporations opening up markets and creating consumers on a global scale. More specifically, he suggests that this movement consequently imposes the English language on foreign workers so that the production, circulation, and consumption of capital remain under the control of Britain and the United States. Thus, as the neoliberal market increasingly dominates social policies, nation-states focus more on English language education than on the promotion of multilingualism. Coleman (2011) has shown that there is an increasing trend to introduce English from the early grades of schooling in developing nations, without considering sociopolitical, educational, and linguistic ramifications in local contexts. Since nation-building discourses in developing countries are heavily influenced by a neoliberal ideology of economic development, countries such as Nepal, India, and Nicaragua have become increasingly focused on English language teaching rather than promoting equity through multilingual or home language education (e.g., Coelho & Henze, 2014; Mohanty, 2006; Phyak, 2016).

The new political economy in the current international neoliberal regime has clearly influenced language policy and practices across situations and sites. In critically examining English language dominance in Europe, Phillipson (2008) argues that "there is an unresolved tension between maintaining the autonomy of national languages and the hegemonic consolidation of English both in the supranational institutions and within each state" (p. 261). The colonial legacy of English in countries such as India (Ramanathan, 2013), the Philippines (Tupas, 2015), and South Africa (Orman, 2008) have served to maintain and/or advance English in the name of globalization (Annamalai, 2003). Local language policies and practices as shaped by global language ideologies, known as *glocalization*, travel along unregulated flows of ideas, people, technology, money, and media across countries (see Coleman, 2011). These policies tend to emphasize—implicitly and explicitly—the teaching of English from the early grades of schooling without benefit of understanding the educational and social ramifications of this action.

Drawing on the world-system theory, Pan (2011) analyzes how China's emphasis on English language education is deeply influenced by economic globalization. For example, the 2003 Chinese "English Curriculum Requirements at Compulsory Education Stage" states that "…the informatization of social life and economic globalization have increased the importance of English…English has become the most widely used language in various sectors of human life" (cited in Pan, 2011, p. 249). Building on Hu (2005), Pan (2011) argues that China has to focus on English due to the increased competitive nature of the global market. Beyond the state-level, China faces "…unprecedented challenges to sustained economic development, an imperative for integration into the global economy, internationalization and technological development" (p. 250). Pan (2011), however, contends that the neutralization of English as a language of economic globalization is an example of "ideological hegemony" (Blommaert, 2006) that occurs when there is complete dominance of one assumption or worldview over another. Hegemonic policies and practices are considered the natural condition of a social order (Fairclough, 2006) that obscures sociopolitical relations embedded within ideological practices. For example, Pan (2011) argues that the de facto compulsory study of English "puts young individuals in a passive position" through which those who are less proficient in English may be excluded from further education and career advancement.

The taken-for-granted symbolic capital of English-as-a-commodity in education has contributed to widening the gap between the lower-/middle- and elite social classes. Drawing on language policies from the postcolonial contexts of India and South Africa (and the countries where English is taught as a foreign and additional language), Ricento (2015) argues that English language expansion both as subject and medium of instruction has promoted a gap between the poor and rich. He claims that "English is often promoted by its advocates as a social 'good' with unquestioned instrumental value; yet access to quality English-medium education in low-income countries is mostly restricted to those with sufficient economic means to pay for it" (Ricento, 2015, p. 1). More importantly, Ricento argues that there is no correlation between English language learning and participating in the international job market as is reproduced in dominant language policy discourses (also see Park & Wee, 2012). In the postcolonial context of India, for example, the legitimacy of English as a dominant language of education has reproduced historically rooted class-based inequalities. While a relatively small percentage of the Indian population takes advantage of the English medium education policy, a large number of people still lack literacy and consequently experience high levels of poverty (Annamalai, 2003; Ramanathan, 2005). Ricento (2015) further argues that as the global spread of English in education disproportionately benefits people who possess the appropriate credentials of fluency in the appropriate English discourse, billions of people in the current world system are left far behind owing to lack of appropriate education credentials and required language skills. Other studies (e.g., Bale, 2015; Block, 2014) show that English language spread has created an increasing gap between the rich and poor that exacerbates existing unequal power realties.

Piller and Cho's (2013) notion of "structure of competition" provides a critical perspective in understanding how neoliberal ideology in education creates unequal access to resources. Their analysis of the English medium of instruction policy in South Korean higher education shows how neoliberal ideology created a structure of competition in education that eventually legitimized standardized testing and the symbolic dominance of English. In critiquing the role of the World Bank and International Monetary Fund in covertly imposing an ideology of competition as a benchmark of university ranking, Piller and Cho specifically argue that "the spread of English is not a result of the free linguistic market but of a "systematic, organized, and orchestrated policy" (p. 38). Their analysis shows that very few students benefit from the institutionalization of English "as one of the terrains where individuals and institutions must compete to be deemed meritorious" (p. 39). Piller and Cho (2013) suggest that "while the benefits of English proficiency to some individuals in South Korea are obviously substantial, the costs of English to the common good are potentially much larger" (p. 39). They argue that English policies have suppressed *freedom of speech* by no longer recognizing the centrality of Korean in education; creating the heavy financial burden of developing English language institutions; and producing student anxiety and fear of failure (often may lead to suicide) among both educators and students.

Neoliberalism has also been shown to reproduce racial/ethnic inequalities and oppression. Lipman (2011) argues that the post-Civil Rights era rejected discourses of "'race" and "racial oppression" as a social issue in the United States. Neoliberal discourses subsequently assumed that racial inequalities can be ameliorated through individual entrepreneurship, freedom of choice, and accountability. Such "colorblind" discourses disinvest the state from taking responsibility in addressing deeply ingrained racial inequalities in education, employment, access to higher education, and political involvement. In fact, the de-racialization of the racial issue is the "silent partner of the market" (Brown, 2007, cited in Lipman, 2011). McNally (2011) equates neoliberalism with racial capitalism in arguing that

> Capitalism remains as racialized as ever...one of the principal manifestations of racial capitalism today is the regulation and persecution of migrant laborers. Millions of poor workers of color from the Global South are hounded, arrested, detained, bullied, mercilessly exploited in homes, sweatshops and on farms, denied social services and civil rights, and subject to racist attacks.
>
> (pp. 143–144)

Social and educational language policies often reproduce standard language ideologies that either ignore or label minoritized languages educationally and socially "deficient". Flores and Rosa (2015) argue that negatively judging language practices (such as creoles, language varieties and accent) of ethnic minoritized people is indeed reflective of racial discrimination, which they call a *raciolinguistic ideology*. This ideology is present globally such as with the displacement of indigenous languages in Nepali schools and other public spheres as the government ignores their previous mandate to promote language diversity (Phyak, 2016). As Nepali national educational policies and practices continue to reproduce inequitable global discourses such as English-as-a-global-language, a competitive job market, and technological advancement, indigenous languages receive less attention in schools that are controlled through high-caste/social elite ideological hegemony (see Giri, 2010, 2011).

We argue here the importance of focusing on how neoliberal interpretations of language policies contribute to "creative destruction" (Harvey, 2005) of linguistic diversity, minoritized languages, and nonstandard forms of languages. In promoting the ideology of language commodification, neoliberalism not only creates unequal access to production, distribution, and consumption of linguistic and educational resources but weakens a sense of "collectivity, social responsibility, equality, and solidarity" (Lipman, 2011, p. 10). Thus, indigenous and other socioeconomically challenged peoples are often dispossessed from the benefits of utilizing their own languages, cultures, knowledge systems, and literacy practices. Given language policies are dictated by the economic market, schools and universities develop policies that are ultimately defined as spaces to produce "human capital" in which market and educational knowledge and skills are repackaged as marketable entities that can be bought and sold (see Holborow, 2015).

Engaging Language Policy Agents in Ideological Analysis

The foregoing discussion reveals language policy as "a site of ideological struggle" (Kroskrity, 2009); that is, a contact zone of multiple ideologies that represent specific sociopolitical, cultural, and historical belief systems. The two major emergent issues of concern involve, first, the growing influence of neoliberalism in language policy and practices in education and, second, the tension between monolingual/standard language ideologies and increasing plurilingualism due to human transnational flows. While communities and schools are becoming increasingly linguistically and culturally diverse, dominant language policies and practices in education and other public spheres continue to legitimate monolingual ideologies. We hold that language policy development involves ideological meanings grounded in particular sociopolitical interests (Farr & Song, 2011). What is needed then is the means by which to engage language policy agents in understanding "ideological complexes" (Blommaert, 2009) that impact language policies and practices. Thus, all language policy-making participants—parents, students, teachers, communities, and administrators—must be included in critical analysis so that they have the means by which to achieve "ideological clarification" (Kroskrity, 2009) toward "ideological becoming" (Bakhtin, 1981) that promotes appropriate and just language policies. While education scholars and political scientists may have access to ideological clarification, all those impacted by inequitable ideologies require support toward gaining ideological awareness. This evolving critical consciousness can provide all concerned with access to information that can subsequently inform resistance to inequitable educational practices (see Ball, 2000a, 2000b).

Ruiz's (1984) conceptualization of three language orientations—language as problem, language as right, and language as resource—presents an ideology of educational and language equity that has long provided understanding of how minoritized languages and multilingual practices can be understood in public spheres. When national governments take on monolingual language policies, they most often view multilingualism as a problem rather than a right and resource. Language education scholars hold that, on the contrary, multilingual education policies recognize home languages as valuable resources toward equitable education and access to social services (Conteh & Meier, 2014; García, 2009; Hajek & Slaughter, 2015; May, 2014). Engaging in ideological analysis involves building critical awareness of dominant/hegemonic and multilingual ideologies that shape language policies and practices. This is best achieved through involving all education participants in critically examining policy intent and practice in relation to power, equality and social justice.

Critical and ethnographic language policy studies since the early 1990s (e.g., Davis, 1990, 1991; McCarty, 2011; Tollefson, 2013) have focused on ideological analysis in critiquing language policies. Davis' (1994) ethnographic study in multilingual Luxembourg explored language policy and planning in relation to sociopolitical and economic dynamics. More specifically, her study closely examined language policy at the intersection of language education policies and class-based language use. She found that elite and middle-class students tended to have extensive experience with learning and using the French and German school languages in addition to Luxembourgish while working-class students most often used Luxembourgish only in the home and community. Thus, lower-class students were greatly disadvantaged in efforts to "catch up" to their multilingual peers. In viewing language policy equity as part of the larger sociopolitical structure, Tollefson (1991) similarly took a historical-structural approach in examining how language policies are linked with historical oppression and structural inequalities. Tollefson (1991, 2006, 2013) and Davis (1994, 2009, 2014) have also critiqued language policies that serve the interests of dominant social groups who control political, educational, and economic resources. While historical-structural analysis provides a critical perspective in which to understand oppressive sociopolitical policies and practices connected with language issues, it does not necessarily ameliorate human agency in transforming historical-structural inequalities (see Johnson, 2009, 2013).

Recent ethnographic studies have revealed the centrality of ideology in language policy creation, interpretation, and implementation (Johnson, 2013; McCarty, 2011). Ethnographic studies have focused on multiple ideologies of different actors and analyzed how these ideologies shape language policies and practices on the ground (Johnson, 2013). While it is important to have a critical understanding of multiple language ideologies, to our knowledge ethnographic studies up until now have not engaged in ideological analysis toward ideological clarification and political activism (Fishman, 2001; Kroskrity, 2009). In other words, there is a lack of studies that look at ways in which participants can gain critical awareness about language ideologies that support or challenge discriminatory language policies and practices that, implicitly or explicitly, affect their lives and society as a whole (Davis, 2014; Davis & Phyak, 2015). In the remainder of this chapter, we explore the possibilities of engaged ideological analysis. This emancipatory approach builds on the work of critical theorists across disciplines including Freire (1970), Bakhtin (1981), Fine (2006, 2009), Kroskrity (2009), and Stoudt, Fox, and Fine (2011).

Awakening a Sense of Injustice: Naming Discriminatory Ideologies

Stoudt, Fox, and Fine (2011) suggest that awakening a sense of injustice "unveils and provokes critical consciousness and actions" among the marginalized and those who serve them (also Deutsch, 1974). Through drawing on Freire's (1970) *Pedagogy of the Oppressed*, scholars, educators, and advocates can engage in promoting social justice at local, national, and/or global levels. Advocates of social justice such as Peter McLaren, Ira Shor, Henry Giroux, Henry Levin, Pierre Bourdieu, bell hooks, Michelle Fine, and Antonio Gramsci critically explore social inequalities such as those associated with gender, class, ethnicity, race, and nationality. While critiquing unequal power relations and hierarchical structures in education, these scholars call for democratic models that address inequities that impact students, parents, teachers, communities, and others toward transformative action.

An engaged approach to ideological analysis first and foremost pays attention to raising participants' awareness of the conditions of their own oppression—historical and contemporary—by engaging them in critical dialogue (see Chapter 3; Gegeo & Watson-Gegeo, 2013), participatory action research (Fine, 2006; Warren & Mapp, 2011), counter-narratives (Lee, 2009, 2014), awareness-raising workshops (Davis & Phyak, 2015), and in-depth interviews and focus group discussions (Davis, 2009; Phyak & Bui, 2014). The foremost action in engaged ideological analysis then is to create and provide participants with a dialogic space in which they are exposed to multiple and contradictory ideologies. Participants are then encouraged to interrogate their own ideologies and the sociopolitical meanings of neoliberal and other harmful ideologies while drawing on alternative ideologies toward praxis— that is, reflection and action (Freire, 1970).

Fine and Weis' (2003) work, although not directly related to language policy, provides a blueprint for engaging participants in ideological analysis. With an aim to transform inequalities in the US public schools from the bottom up, Fine and Weis focus on dialogue, which they call "extraordinary conversation," as a major tool for engaging teacher, educators, students, and parents in resisting harmful ideologies that embrace racial, ethnic, gender, language, and class discrimination. Their engaged work highlights two major steps: understanding scenes of silencing, and engaging participants in extraordinary conversations. Scenes of silencing involve critical analysis of how social hierarchies are reproduced in US public schools. After documenting oppressive educational policies and practices, Fine and Weis engage in conversation through which youth, teachers, communities, and parents come together to critically analyze existing conditions of oppression and engage in identifying possibilities for social transformation. In these conversations, subalterns interrogate power relations, build critical consciousness, and construct agency toward transforming inequitable policies and practices.

Gegeo and Watson-Gegeo (2013) also build on Freire's (1970, 1998) critical praxis approach in engaging Solomon Islands indigenous youth and villagers in critical dialogue. Considering dominant language policy as an ideological construct interlocked with larger sociopolitical and economic policies, Gegeo and Watson-Gegeo (2013) take a dialogic approach in drawing indigenous youth and villagers into critical reflection on existing linguistic, political, economic, and education policies and practices. These villagers subsequently name Western neoliberal ideology of development and education as major forces in creating ethnic tension, unemployment, mass migration, social instability, crime, and low educational achievement. In identifying indigenous epistemologies in education and economic enterprises through critical dialogue, youth and villagers further commit to creating social and educational policies that embrace local indigenous languages, identities, and epistemologies.

Lee (2009, 2014) utilizes a counter-narrative method in engaging Navajo and Pueblo youth in analyses of contested ideologies underlying language policies and practices in the United States. In drawing on *Critical Race Theory* and counter-narratives, Lee encourages youth to embrace the stories of their own lived language experiences of frustration concerning increased English language shift as well as the continual struggle to reclaim their heritage language identity in the face of hegemonic language policies and practices. Through counter-storytelling, youth identify tension among dominant ideologies, their own language practices, and worldviews about languages policies. Through becoming ideologically clear about what constitutes an equitable language policy, these indigenous youth realize the injustice of a modern neoliberal conception of development as discriminatory ideology. For example, Pueblo college youth Daniel criticizes the absence of programs and policies that support minoritized languages and argues that "people have ranked other issues such as economic development, infrastructure development, blood quantum, and personal conflict as more important than preserving our language" (Lee, 2009, p. 316). This engaged process consequently led to youth's "critical Indigenous consciousness" toward reclaiming linguistic and cultural identities. Building on Freire (1970), Lee (2009) further defines critical indigenous consciousness "as an awareness of the historical and broad oppressive conditions that have influenced current realities of Indigenous people's lives" (p. 318).

Phyak's (2016) engaged ethnographic work additionally focuses on building critical consciousness among indigenous youth, villagers, and teachers of language ideologies that shape current language policies and practices in Nepal. In also drawing on Freire's (1970) critical consciousness approach, he adopts multiple methods (e.g., collaborative ethnography, focus group discussion, in-depth interviews, workshops, and participatory observation) in engaging Limbu youth, villagers, and teachers in dialogue that interrogates multiple ideologies in terms of how they support or constrain the use of indigenous languages in education and other public spheres. He first explores participants' views about indigenous language policies, national Nepali language policy, and neoliberal imposed English. The participants reveal ambivalent ideological positions given that most participants were unaware of how monolingual ideologies—linguistic nationalism and English-as-a-global language—were linked with sociopolitical, linguistic, and education discrimination. He then engaged youth, parents, and teachers in observing language practices and policies in the school, home, and community. Each observation was followed by reflective dialogue in which villagers and youth interrogated language ideologies and practices that they observed. This dialogue became a contact zone of authoritative discourses (legitimate or official discourses that were embraced by the dominant public sphere) and internally persuasive discourses (language practices that are not fully recognized in the dominant public sphere). Through participating in sociopolitical dialogue with participants, Phyak was able to raise awareness of how official language policies such as a monolingual English language policy can have negative educational, sociopolitical and economic ramifications for the indigenous and poor. He further presented research that acknowledges the advantages of multilingual schooling that forefronts learning through home languages while adding languages of educational and/or economic benefit (e.g., Cummins, 2006; García, 2009). In commenting on the legitimacy of the Limbu language in the school and community, a Limbu villager observes that "our language is important for our identity and culture…but what can we do? The state didn't recognize it. The state wanted to kill our language and culture. Still our languages aren't taught in school. This is injustice, no?" In the same way, indigenous youth consider monolingual policies and practices as "tools to suppress their home languages and cultures." By acquiring knowledge of both harmful neoliberal ideologies and multilingual benefits, these participants came to own their own perspectives and, thus, a sense of "ideological becoming" (Bakhtin, 1981). The next step in ideological becoming is to transform education policy from neoliberal hegemony to language of empowerment and equity.

Denaturalizing and Transforming Hegemonic Ideologies

With increased critical awareness of social injustice in dominant language policies and practices, engaged ideological analysis provides communities, youth, and educators with the tools to denaturalize deeply ingrained hegemonic language ideologies (Hymes, 1980, 1991, 1996). Scholars from across disciplines ranging from education to environmentalism have drawn on Freire's critical consciousness and dialogic method toward realizing situated emancipatory practices. Kemmis and McTaggart (2005) argue that social justice, collaboration, and activism are at the heart of participatory approaches that confirm Freire's position that activism, without critical reflection, does not contribute to liberating education. Kemmis and McTaggart (2005) further suggest drawing on Freire's dialogic methods of critical consciousness raising and other neo-Marxist approaches to social justice, community development, and activism. These scholars specifically promote a participatory action research (PAR) approach that engages all participants across the range of situations, locations, and ideologies in the act of uncovering underlying inequalities and oppression. PAR further seeks commitment to social, economic, and political development in addressing the needs and opinions of people marginalized by discrimination and oppression. More specifically, this research approach is considered a collaborative, emancipatory, reflexive, critical, and transformative social process in which marginalized communities and individuals are provided with a "communicative space" in which to interact with one another and build collective agency and solidarity for social action (Habermas, 1996; Kemmis & McTaggart, 2005). An engaged approach takes on these characteristics while centrally focused on the processes rather than the products of transformative participatory research. While researchers draw on a repertoire of methods that include Freirean, critical ethnographic, PAR and other methods, the focus is on collaborative design and implementation toward ongoing consciousness-raising and productive action. Thus, rather than reporting findings, an engaged research approach attends to the social, linguistic, cultural, and political through portraying the processes of situated engagement and transformation of policies and practices.

From a different perspective and through other means, social psychology scholar Michelle Fine draws on the Freirean approach and PAR in challenging injustice rooted in dominant educational policies and sociopolitical discourses. In considering PAR "democratic engagement", Fine calls on researchers to address social justice through recognition of distributive, procedural, and public rights. In theorizing methods of research for studying oppression, Fine (2006) argues that deep-seated oppression in our everyday life often goes unnoticed, partly because of its nonviolent nature. She cites Harvey's (1999) concept of "civilized oppression" to demonstrate the unconscious character of marginalization. Civilized oppression refers to

> [...]the vast and deep injustices some groups suffer as a consequence of often unconscious assumptions and reactions of well meaning people in ordinary interactions which are supported by the media and cultural stereotypes as well as the structural features of bureaucratic hierarchies and market mechanism.
>
> (Harvey, 1999, pp. 3–4)

The question embedded in this observation is how can we "awaken a sense of injustice" in the face of hidden agendas and crippling despair? Fine (2006) urges us "to situate ourselves, among other actors, in civic struggles for justice, through the courts, community organizing, scholarships, and public writing" (p. 87). In challenging the notion of "objectivity," Fine engages students in critical conversation on how to "gather counter-hegemonic perspectives and standpoints that challenge dominant views, rather than conducting research that reproduces dominant ideologies—even as these dominant views may be narrated by some of the most oppressed people in the nation" (p. 90). Fine's engaged work further involves engaging students in critical historical analysis toward uncovering "the collective lies" told as history while exploring "untold stories" that may be reclaimed as collective identity (Fine, 2006, p. 92; also see Martin-Baró, 1994). Through this process, students develop critical understanding of how power is unequally distributed; ways in which social inequalities are reproduced; and the means by which agency can be reclaimed. A similar approach has been successfully used among indigenous peoples through language and culture reclamation and maintenance in education and other public spaces (McCarty, 2003; McCarty & Wyman, 2009; Smith, 2012; Wyman, 2012). Fine (2006) and Freire (1970) among others have argued that critical understanding of historical inequalities *with*, not *for*, the oppressed is necessary in order to resist and transform inequitable policies. Thus, we hold that engaged ethnography is not just a method of data collection; rather it is a democratic form of knowledge production in which the wisdom, voices, and ideologies of the oppressed are recognized through the research process (also Davis, Phyak, & Bui, 2012).

Stoudt, Fox, and Fine (2011) specifically draw on PAR as a form of engagement with students in questioning injustices and analyzing how social inequalities are reproduced. Through their research, youth created "contact zones" (Torre, 2005) in which they brought varied expertise together and designed new ways in which to document the impact of social policies on their lives while supporting social movement against subordination and toward a sense of justice. In their *Rockford Bullying Study* and *Polling for Justice* projects, Stoudt et al. (2011) worked with relatively privileged youth who "bear witness" to social injustices and are engaged in actions to awaken critical consciousness of the responsibilities of the elite. They further work in collaboration with working-class or otherwise marginalized youth toward gaining collective awareness of how their lives are affected by poverty, marginalization, and neoliberal social policies. Facilitators engage youth in four major activities: naming and mapping unequal distribution of opportunities; denaturalizing unjust distribution of opportunities; making visible the interdependence and circuit of oppression that impact society; and engaging in collective research to provoke a sense of responsibility toward social change.

In the *Rockford Bullying Study*, faculty and student research teams representing the Upper School of Rockport, an elite predominately white private school, worked together in examining how masculine privilege is reproduced through bullying. Student researchers found four major types of bullying: teasing, intimidation, hazing, and fighting. To address this existential reality, school faculty volunteered to act as on-the-ground researchers in developing interview protocols and interviewing other faculty members about student findings. Together, teachers and students analyzed data and communicated their findings to the larger school community. Through this process, students developed a deepening awareness of how bullying represented a "highly competitive culture" that elite colleges have promoted in the form of "a mission for privilege and power" within a competitive and capitalistic education marketplace. The students also understood bullying as an expression of masculinity that subsequently reflected existing social power relations. After naming bullying as the reproduction of social inequalities, students and teachers engaged in denaturalizing so-called civilized oppression through critical dialogue. In their collaborative effort to analyze the data, they began to develop a deepening awareness that white, private school, upper-class, and male privilege are masked by a "false sense of merit"; that is, "a sense of earned and therefore justified success linked to one's personal attributes without recognizing how institutionalized advantages are linked with others' disadvantages" (Stoudt et al., 2011, p. 173). Student researcher Sara suggests that students in Rockford "believe they are so much higher up than the public schools of anybody around here that they feel like the [college] competition for them are these kids in their classes" (Stoudt et al., 2011, p. 173). Similarly, Mary (a faculty researcher) observes that

> [t]hey always put down community college ... It is so elitist. Our boys are so unaware of the fact that the reason they have all these amazing choices is that they have been handed so many advantages. If we were judging on merit they'd be damn lucky to be at community college.
>
> (p. 173)

This form of engaged research created collaborative space for students and teachers to challenge their own privilege, become aware of the fact that they themselves are contributing to social injustice and hierarchies, and take responsibility for equity transformation. John (a student researcher) argues "these aren't like special people with high moral standards; they are just everyday people like doing what everybody else does. It is the same exact type of people ...to like public school" (p. 174). From their interpersonal communication and development of increased critical understanding of structures, ideological practices, and the negative impact of current school policies, faculty and student researchers began a mission to stop bullying. Student researchers planned for interventions such as public awareness raising through town hall meetings and dialogue with other students, faculty members, and the larger community. This process subsequently engaged students and teachers in transforming a hegemonic school culture to one of equity and respect. The project suggests that active participant engagement through PAR and other engaged forms of research not only challenges the researcher-researched dichotomy but resists distributive and procedural injustices.

The *Echoes of Brown* (Fine et al., 2004) project raised awareness of equity issues through engaging youth in unveiling inequality in documenting and performing the legacy of *Brown vs. Board of Education*. Through a series of "research camps" in New York and New Jersey, Fine and colleagues trained more than 100 high school youth to investigate the "opportunity gap". These youth joined researchers from the Graduate Center of City University to study youth perspectives on experiences of race- and class-based injustice within and across their schools. Youth from diverse backgrounds investigated the history of struggles for desegregation and analyzed current educational opportunities and inequalities in terms of race, ethnicity, and class. While youth learned research skills and social justice theories from experts, they shared evidence they found of instances of educational (in)justice. The project further drew on an interdisciplinary team of historians, lawyers, researchers, and activists as experts in interpreting the history of race and class struggles in public education; the *Brown vs. Board of Education* decision on racial equity; civil rights movements and struggles for educational justice for English-language learners; and learners with disabilities and lesbian/ gay youth. Thus, youth and adult experts collaboratively designed, critiqued, edited, revised, and carried out research agendas. Youth researchers interviewed high school students on issues of race and class (in)justice in schools across the nation. They also explored matters of equity such as bilingualism and gender identities; met with state legislators, historians, journalists, and activists; and reviewed how federal policies have discriminated against poor and working-class children. Youth and adults further analyzed both quantitative and qualitative data and documented structures and policies that produce inequalities and the ideologies that justify opportunity gaps.

The findings of this comprehensive study also revealed that racial and class-based inequalities are embedded in high-stakes testing and unequal suspension and segregation policies. This information was subsequently disseminated by youth and adult researchers in a range of academic and community settings and across diverse forums. Kareem (African-American youth) and Kendra (white youth), for example, began to take on an activist position by challenging school injustices they witnessed. Through collaborative research, this group achieved a collective understanding of the policies, practices, and consequences of inequity and subsequently began to reimagine schools as sites of engaged social justice (Torre & Fine, 2011, p. 115). As a public message of equity, this project involved youth, community elders, social scientists, artists, dancers, choreographers, and videographers in producing *Echoes of Brown* based on the landmark 1954 *Brown vs. Board of Education* anti-decimation action that desegregated schooling in the United States. In sum, this project contributed to raising critical awareness among youth and concerned others about social injustice. The project further argues that marginalized/oppressed youth *can* engage in "sharp critique and knowledge" of inequitable social relations and, thus, bring out liberating transformation.

Guishard (2009) further draws on both Paulo Freire and PAR toward enhancing critical consciousness among African American and Latino parents/

youth in challenging multiple aspects of social inequalities surrounding education, gender, race, and economy in South Bronx, New York City. She defines critical consciousness as "the continuous process by which parent organizers and youth researchers nurture capacities to identify, perceive, and name the structures, policies, and practices of educational oppression and how they engaged in actions to radically transform these conditions" (p. 93). Critical consciousness is nonlinear and deeply rooted in people's lived experiences over time and space. Guishard (2009) uses critical self-reflection, individual oral histories, participant observation, focus groups, and archival analysis to explore (1) the conditions under which African American and Latino parents struggle for their children's equality and quality of education and (2) ways in which parents can draw on participatory research toward their own evolving political consciousness and action. By engaging in issue meetings that promote leadership development, public accountability, and direct action campaigns, these parents developed "activist parenting" that helps their children to build the positive self-image needed to counter demeaning living conditions and foster school achievement. Issue meetings provided "a safe space" for parents to share their stories of struggles, frustration, and a feeling of powerlessness with school agendas while they simultaneously take on active advocacy for educational justice.

The engaged approaches described here go beyond traditional ethnography that assumes knowledge and interpretation lie in the hands of the researcher. Thus, ideologies, knowledge, and skills of the researched often go unrecognized, even with member checking and other forms of validating findings. In addition, we hold that unequal distribution of knowledge through failure to actively engage participants can readily become for them a dehumanizing and possibly colonizing endeavor (Fine, 2009; Smith, 2012). In essence, procedural injustice occurs when participants are excluded from participation in determining and carrying out research agendas. While exclusion potentially reproduces dominant language ideologies, policies, and practices, engaged research seeks to uncover the "circuits of dispossession" (Fine & Ruglis, 2009)—the ways in which privilege and disadvantage are linked at individual and societal levels. This suggests critical examination of how people are dispossessed of assets and rights, what Harvey (2004, p. 2) calls "accumulation by dispossession." Harvey suggests that neoliberal capitalist policies are promoted primarily through privatization, financialization, management, and manipulation of crises, and state redistribution. More specifically, there is growing "uneven geographic development" and consequently a global gap between the wealthy and poor through, for example, private ownership of community water and public spaces along with inequitable access to housing and education (Stoudt et al., 2011). Harvey further holds that global capital is accumulated by multinational corporations and thus "we're talking about the taking away of universal rights and the privatization of them so it [becomes] your particular responsibility, rather than the responsibility of the state" (Harvey, 2004, p. 2).

PAR and other forms of engaged research are designed to situate critiques from the "margins" (hooks, 1994) and to explore alternate possibilities for justice (Anzaldúa, 1987; Torre & Fine, 2004). Engaged methods are intended to "shatter the false consensus of neoliberal institutional life by challenging the everyday banality and seeming inevitability of injustice" (Fine & Torre, 2006, p. 255). PAR engages with multiple stories and counter-stories that are left unheard and ignored under dominant social control. Cammarota and Fine (2008) and Morrell (2008), among others, portray youth engagement in critical dialogue and activism to resist and transform social injustice in education. They engage youth in understanding complex power relations and histories of struggle, analyzing consequences of oppression, and performing action to challenge these for their own liberation. They argue that youth have the capacity and agency to analyze social contexts … and challenge the forces impeding their own voices and liberation. In sum, we argue for an engaged language policy approach that goes beyond identification of linguicism toward an interdisciplinary and engaged approach to addressing human welfare challenges.

3
ENGAGED ETHNOGRAPHY AS TRANSFORMATIVE LANGUAGE POLICY PROCESSES

Language policy studies have drawn on a range of research methods in investigating the historical genesis of policies and practices; situated contexts of language use; and evolving sociopolitical dynamics that shape language ideologies, policies, and practices (Canagarajah, 2005; Davis, 2014; Hult & Johnson, 2015). Hornberger and Johnson (2007) have argued that ethnography of language policy sheds light on how official top-down language policies and planning (LPP) play out in particular contexts, including interaction with bottom-up language policies that reveal multiple voices, covert motivation, embedded ideologies, and intended and unintended consequences of policy development. This approach further seeks to address structural power relations and agency of language policy actors by recognizing the importance of local policy discourses (Johnson, 2013; Johnson & Ricento, 2013; Hornberger & Johnson, 2007; McCarty, 2011). Yet while ethnographers report research concerning on-the-ground language policies and practices, descriptions of the politics, processes, and intent of language research often go unreported.

We portray here ways in which participants and researchers collectively engage in transforming complex discriminatory language ideologies and practices, especially in peripheral communities of marginalized populations (Davis, 2014; Phyak & Bui, 2014). More specifically, we argue that all language policy actors must be provided with engaged space for achieving agency through resistance to global and local hegemonic ideologies. This perspective suggests that articulation of the overall *process* of engagement and activism among those directly involved promotes egalitarian language policies. While ethnographic studies of social and educational rights have contributed much in the way of descriptive analysis of action and outcomes, a more fully articulated engaged language policy and practices approach can support language education transformation. We begin with a historical overview of critical and political ethnographic research toward informing engaged ethnographic studies.

Critical, Political and Engaged Research

Torre and Fine (2011) report Wormser and Selltiz's (1951) "community self-survey" as the first critical/political research approach designed, in this case, to challenge racial injustice in the United States. In their *How to Conduct a Community Self-Survey of Civil Rights*, Wormser and Selltiz (1951) introduced self-survey as a strategy to provoke individuals and communities to question and move beyond their individual lived experiences to a broader understanding of civil rights in their community based on objective evidence (p. 1, cited in Torre & Fine, 2011, p. 108). These scholars further argued that full participation of relevant communities and use of democratic practices throughout the research process must be ensured. Thus, in utilizing a community self-survey approach, individuals from different racial/ethnic backgrounds were expected to work together in exploring social issues and planning social justice action. Popularly used in the United States throughout the 1950s, this approach asked community member participants to invest in documenting and transforming discriminatory practices rather than directly grappling with prejudicial attitudes. The community surveys further relied on "local knowledge" to unearth the "discriminatory practices and policies being followed in the community" (Lambert & Cohen, 1949, p. 48). For example, their Montclair Audit project involved a number of studies such as white and black students exploring restaurant practices, real estate agents studying housing policies and practices, and truck drivers collecting information about their customers' biracial practices (see Lambert & Cohen, 1949).

As early as the 1920s, Franz Boas began to lay the groundwork for linking anthropology with public service, particularly through critiquing racism. Margaret Mead's anthropological work in the 1930s led to expanding the role of anthropologists through addressing pragmatic problems associated with human welfare such as issues of race, housing, and pollution. However, during and after World War II, activism was overridden by the pressure to (mis) use anthropology and, more specifically, ethnographic research for military purposes (see Low & Merry, 2010). It was not until the 1960s that an activist anthropological perspective re-emerged, most significantly through association with US Vietnam War protests and the US Civil Rights movement. The 1968 special issue of *Current Anthropology* proclaimed the need for ethnographers to take social responsibility in conducting critical analyses by challenging pervasive imperialism and racial discrimination. That issue specifically promoted insider anthropology focusing on African American ethnographic critique

(Low & Merry, 2010). Feminist anthropology also emerged at this time as a result of increasing demands for recognition of women's participation, active engagement, and ongoing transformation toward achieving sociopolitical rights equal to those of men (Susser, 2010). Hymes' (1969) *Reinventing Anthropology* further called for reorienting the field of anthropology from description of the mundane to activism for social justice and equality. More specifically, Hymes encouraged anthropologists, as committed members of the community, to take a strong anti-imperialist stance and invest in empowering communities to participate in social movements through direct action.

In the mid-1980s, cultural critique was increasingly acknowledged as a form of ethnographic engagement. George Marcus and Michael Fischer's (1986) *Anthropology as Cultural Critique* and James Clifford and George Marcus's (1986) *Writing Culture* proposed addressing multiple voices and social inequalities from deconstructionist and postcolonial/subaltern perspectives (Low & Merry, 2010). By the late 1980s, cultural critique had begun to incorporate advocacy-oriented and collaborative research methods (see Schensul & Schensul, 1992). This approach subsequently considered so-called "informants" as co-researchers and colleagues in challenging structural inequalities and power differentials that operate between the center and periphery of race, ethnicity, gender, and social class. Yet the reconceptualization of anthropology as "public engagement" was not realized until the early 1990s (Forman, 1993). The major aspects of engagement at this time focused on anthropology as a source of social criticism that promoted community engagement, policy as multi-voiced, student active involvement, and ethnographer re-engaging in continuous self-criticism from within the discipline (Low & Merry, 2010; also see Forman, 1993).

From the late 1990s onward, activism and ethically grounded ethnographic research received increasing attention in anthropology. Anthropology progressively served as "a site of resistance" and "political practice" in which social stratification, inequality, injustice, and oppression are challenged and transformed through collaborative ethnography involving social critique, teaching, advocacy, and activism. Critical anthropologists have subsequently influenced scholars across disciplines to engage participants in research processes toward creating public policy (Clarke, 2010, p. 302). Specifically, ethnographers are called upon to be social critics in documenting efforts to resist cultural, linguistic, and political violence and engage in social equity transformation. For example, Clarke (2010) criticizes worldwide US army deployment and subsequently asserts that ethnographers should document the realities of "social power-enfranchisement, inequality, and power abuse in order to intervene before and during conflict contexts" (p. 310). Thus, collaborative action, social mobilization, and multiple forms of documentation have all been recognized as strategic methods. From an engaged perspective, ethnography is a "technology of knowledge and power whose methods can capture the complexities of ruptures and entanglements or histories of violence of all forms and suggest lessons that might be learned from these complex social contexts" (Clarke, 2010, p. 310). Engaged ethnography further addresses "the basis for social injustice by taking legible public positions within relevant fields of social and political power" (Clarke, 2010, p. 311). In this sense, engaged ethnography is "the site of the convergence of an engaged practice of knowledge making and sharing with a highly circumscribed decision-making process" that questions who shares knowledge under whose terms and for what purposes. Clarke (2010) also argues that "these queries are vital for exploring the ways we ask and answer questions and for the ways that we revisit those intellectual and practical histories that have influenced our practices and enabled various sites of inequality to flourish" (p. 311).

Going beyond traditional "thick description" of a phenomenon or an event, Hymes (1980, p. 99) defined ethnography as an open-ended and democratic method of inquiry that has the potential for "helping to overcome division of society into those who know and those who are known." Focusing on the importance of engagement and activism in research, Hymes (1969) further proposed an anti-imperialist stance and reiterated the need for researchers to "go beyond the academic world and work for communities or movements, even engaging in direct action as a member (of the community)" (p. 56). As Freire (1970) suggests, those who intervene should build a sense of trust and caring with participants in dialogic processes of policy reform. Hymes (1980) further claims that a good ethnographer "entails trust and confidence…that requires some narrative accounting…and is an extension of a universal form of personal knowledge" (p. 99). For both Freire and Hymes, the validity of ethnographic data is examined in terms of whether they reflect deep-seated social realities. Highlighting the transformative potential of ethnography, Hymes (1980) further maintains that researchers should focus on how they can help "transform them [social inequalities] through knowledge of the ways in which language is actually organized as a human problem and resources" (p. 56). This goes beyond language policy action research, such as that proposed by Johnson (2013), toward in-depth political activism grounded in Hymesian and Freirean participatory approaches to addressing language and social injustice.

ELP frames and portrays our overall participatory approach as political in nuanced and public ways toward promoting the means by which the dispossessed work to possess the right to research, advocate, and acquire sustainable, equitable, and self-defined honorable ways of learning and living. Like other critical research approaches (Cammarota & Fine, 2008; Fine, 2006; Freire, 1970), ELP places participants at the center of investigations while striving to awaken a sense of injustice among those with material and cultural power. Yet engaged ethnograhy further aims to describe and portray ways in which all concerned individuals and institutions—policy makers, administrators, teachers, parents/community members, students, schools, local organizations—are joined in processes of developing awareness of inequitable ideologies as well as the means by which to challenge inhumane, demeaning, and exclusionary policies and practices from within. We explore here a range of critical and participatory methodologies toward envisioning an engaged ethnographic approach to language education policy-making and practices. We began with an historical overview by Torre and Fine (2011) that provides a comprehensive grounding in past participatory approaches that serve as building blocks for our emerging conceptualization of engaged research and practices approaches. This chapter further revisits the work of pioneer language activists, such as William Labov and Dell Hymes. Through this historical review, we intend to situate our language policy and practices experience and engagement within the context of critical and liberatory approaches.

Engaged Ethnography

Moving ethnography toward an advocacy and activist direction, Low and Merry (2010) introduce and theorize the concept of "engaged anthropology" as an approach to supporting activist work for social change. They argue that an engaged ethnographer pays attention to sharing knowledge and power with communities, to empower them through social critique and collaborative actions and contribute to public policy-making processes. In keeping social equity at the center of ethnographic work, Low and Merry (2010) focus on ethnographers' engagement with communities and individuals as activists who foster social critique toward transforming a host of issues that affect people's lived experiences.

Ethnographic/qualitative researchers have further been influenced by epistemological stances arising from modern and postmodern eras. Yet rather than a chronology of social science shifts (Grbich, 2004), these eras present ongoing melding and crossing over of epistemological, theoretical, and methodological approaches depending on individual and normative institutional views. During the modernist era, anthropologist Hymes (1974) proposed the ethnography of communication in response to the cognitively and post-positivist defined second language acquisition research paradigm. He argued that speech acts and other communicative events cannot be fully understood without attending to culture and context. Hymes' ethnographic social constructivist theories and methods subsequently influenced studies of cross-cultural communication in classrooms (Cazden et al., 1972); participation structure differences between community and classroom interactive norms (Philips, 1983); and comprehensive analysis of sociocultural language and literacy expectations in racially, economically, and culturally diverse communities (Heath, 1983). Yet Hymes also argued against one-sided ethnographic research and reporting; rather, he proposed ethnographic monitoring as a form of research that is processual and highly collaborative. He suggests sharing knowledge about home/school language and social practices among all interested educational actors, including the ethnographer (Hymes, 1991; Van der Aa & Blommaert, 2011). He essentially proposes ongoing mutual inquiry rather than simply "reporting back," given his view that intensive and genuine cooperation is at the heart of ethnographic monitoring (Hymes & Fought, 1981, pp. 10–11). He further argues that "a framework starting with issues identified by teachers, and continuing cooperation may make findings more acceptable and likely to be utilized" (Hymes & Fought, 1981, p. 13).

At about the same time, anthropologist Geertz (1983) brought into question the nature of reality and the centrality of local studies. Geertz suggested that ethnographers explore local situations and acknowledge the interpretive nature of analyses and presentation of findings. He also argued that an interpretive approach implies the blurring of boundaries between the social sciences and humanities. Researchers subsequently have sought new models of truth, method, and (multimodal) representation while increasingly engaging in reflexivity and calling into question issues of gender, class, and race. This blurring of research methods boundaries and terminology has similarly occurred across social science fields and increasingly in applied linguistics. A notable interpretive representation of blurred methods and genres is Anzaldúa's *Borderlands/La Frontera: The New Mestiza* (1987). In this bilingual (Spanish/English) collection of essays and poems, Anzaldúa explores the notion of identity through her own multilingual and sociocultural experiences as Chicana, lesbian, and activist. She challenges traditional and modernist binary, apolitical, monolingual, and scientific representations of social inquiry through using literary venues to define "borders" as an inhabited space and legitimate identity. While applied linguists have not challenged written representations to a similar degree, there has been a growing tendency toward contesting dominant Western or modernist paradigms through alternative (non-Western) knowledge and genre constructions.

An increasing number of ethnographic studies within and across multilingual contexts began to emerge at this time, particularly in the fields of language policy and planning, language learning, and schooling. Ethnographies began to take on a political edge in advocating for equitable language and culture schooling. Hornberger's (1989) language policy and planning work with Quechua communities and McCarty's efforts with the Navajo people (Dick & McCarty, 1992; McCarty, 2002; McCarty & Schaffer, 1992) acknowledged the challenges of indigenous language maintenance and supported bilingual education efforts. Davis (1994) argued for bottom-up language planning that recognizes working-class children's linguistic needs through her ethnographic study of multilingual schooling and class variation in language socialization and use in Luxembourg. Zentella (1997) advocated for multilingual education reform through her ethnographic study of Puerto Rican children in New York that documented the complex linguistic and social character of language use. Huebner and Davis

(1999) focused on LPP sociopolitical perspectives in an edited volume that explored a range of LPP frameworks, politics, and practices in the United States.

In the 1990s and early twenty-first century, postmodernism also began to take hold in SLA and the larger field of applied linguistics. Postmodernism considers the nature of knowledge as multifaceted, locally situated, and time- and context-bound. This philosophical position opposes research assumptions of political neutrality and argues instead for examination of power relations in language and literacy studies. Postmodernism specifically refutes the notion that language can be understood in structuralist terms as a network of systematically linked propositions and coherent organized units. Subsequently, New Literacies Studies scholars (e.g., Gee, 2000) advanced research based on the premise that, rather than a set of static, decontextualized, and discrete skills, literacy is always dynamic, multifaceted, power-laden, and situated in local practices. Applied linguists and socially situated SLA researchers have increasingly focused on language and cultural diversity in investigating multiple communication channels, hybrid textual forms, new local and global social relations, and power relations from ever-evolving, changing, locally, and politically situated perspectives (e.g., Duff, 2004; Kanno, 2003; Lam, 2000; Lin et al., 2002; Norton, 2000; Rampton, 1995; Warschauer, 1999).

Researchers and theorists currently utilize a range of approaches to researching and theorizing social and political meanings that can inform local policies and practices. As previously mentioned, critical scholars such as Pennycook, Phillipson, and Skutnabb-Kangas have long offered textual and social analyses that further understanding of the political and social meanings of actions such as those associated with English imperialism and globalization. LPP specialists such as Shohamy (2006) have further argued for uncovering "hidden agendas" that can "…create language hierarchies, marginalize and exclude groups, and thus lead to the violation of personal rights and undemocratic practices" (p. xvii, also McCarty & Warhol, 2011). Yet Shohamy further suggests the potential of a "dynamic process of multiple discourses for negotiations and battling existing language policies" (p. xvii). She argues that such views "…could lead to the creation of inclusive policies, which are open and dynamic, and where policy and practice closely interact and contribute to a democracy of inclusion, the protection of personal rights, along with strategies of language awareness and activism" (p. xvii).

Lin and Martin (2005) specifically argue for an epistemological shift from critical deconstruction to a critical construction paradigm that addresses decolonization, globalization, and language-in-education policy and practices. From a related but different viewpoint, language scholars such as Alim et al. (2009), Alim (2011), and Pennycook (2010) have taken sociopolitical perspectives into postmodern realms through qualitative descriptions of global to local performative acts in which languages, cultures, and styles, such as hip-hop, are appropriated, integrated, and transformed by youth. More direct transformative actions are found among the growing number of language, literacy, and education specialists (e.g., Alim, 2011; Duncan-Andrade & Morrell, 2008; Luke, 2002) who call for critical and participatory research approaches to addressing inequitable educational outcomes. As discussed in the previous chapter, participatory action research (PAR) has evolved as a collaborative effort among members of social communities and researchers to bring about democratic and emancipatory investigations of processes and outcomes. PAR works toward placing local participants at the center of investigations while striving to awaken a sense of injustice among those with material and cultural power. Scholar educators such as Ernest Morrell, Michelle Fine, and Julio Cammarota engage in and describe PAR work with youth in publications such as the edited volume *Revolutionizing Education: Youth Participatory Action Research in Motion* (Cammarota & Fine, 2008).

Luke (2002) argues that the right to research for gaining strategic knowledge necessarily involves emancipatory discourses defined by Freire and colleagues as "forms of talk, writing, and representation that are counter-ideological and act to articulate and configure collective interests in transformative ways" (Luke, 2002, p. 105). Luke specifically calls for critical discourse analysis that provides a positive thesis of productive discourses of power. He suggests that "we would need to begin to capture an affirmative character of culture where discourse is used aesthetically, productively, and for emancipatory purposes" (Luke, 2002, p. 106). Davis (2009) describes agentive discursive practices among youth in Hawai'i that involved investigating multifaceted heritage language and cultural identities while interrogating, challenging, and appropriating academic English practices. Canagarajah's (2005) reflections on future directions for research on multiliteracies emphasize the need for transnational ethnographic studies of students developing rhetorical negotiation strategies that modify, resist, or reorient to expectations for written academic discourse.

The postmodern social science era clearly represents exponential growth in the number and range of interpretive ethnographic and qualitative studies in applied linguistics, in general, and LPP more specifically. Historical boundaries between qualitative research approaches blurred, and notions such as culture, context, and identity are now commonly understood as interpretive, ever-evolving, changing, and locally and politically situated. Yet early twenty-first-century neoliberal ideologies operating in the United States and other nations also indicate movement in neoclassical/autonomous and post-positivist directions in embracing monolingualism or English language spread and standardized curriculum/assessment in public schools and associated research funding (Luke, 2011). While this movement provides support to post-positivist language acquisition scholars, many applied linguistics activists such as Terrence Wiley continue to argue for grounding research, evaluation, and theory in multilingualism, multiculturalism, and local control of education. There has subsequently been a growing social justice movement across disciplines and geographic locations that argues for attending to issues of class, race, gender, and ethnicity as these are associated with language and power (Denzin & Lincoln, 2005; Mallett et al., 2010; colloquium on linking academic and advocacy interests among AAAL members). While researchers argue for social justice-based research within the academy, indigenous and non-Western scholars have engaged in a full-scale attack on Western epistemologies and research methodologies (Smith, 2005, 2012). Indigenous researchers, such as Smith, advocate for decolonizing the academy's scientific practices as they move toward local control of socially situated inquiry. As part of backlash activism from the standpoint of public spheres, socially and politically engaged research and practice are increasingly embraced by postmodern engaged LPP scholar-advocates. In his 2013 edition of *Language Policies in Education: Critical Issues*, Tollefson argues that

> [T]his new (public spheres) direction pays less attention to the state and interstate conflict, and more attention to the margins and borders of states, regions, and communities; less attention to ethnolinguistic groups and more attention to hybrid and multiple identities; less attention to nationalism and more attention to cosmopolitan citizenship; less attention to the sources of social conflict and more attention to mobilities and networks; less attention to the power of corporate capitalism and more attention to alternative media and community organizations; and less attention to the dominance of English and more attention to the rise of new language varieties (including new varieties of English).
>
> (p. 27)

The re-conceptualization of LPP portrays a clear epistemological and analytical shift toward local engagement of subaltern counter-public discourses that challenge the dominant public sphere. The shift further signals the necessity for clearer means in which to chart a situation-specific course toward more equitable LPP that acknowledges local conditions, considers global ideological influence, and works toward locally appropriate responses to language, education, and human welfare needs.

School and classroom language policies that reflect community language use thus support academic achievement while acquiring the primary language/s of instruction. Davis et al. (2005) also document the ways in which students at a high school serving low-income students in Hawai'i reclaimed their heritage languages through classes in Samoan and Ilokano while community language teachers acknowledged use of Hawaiian Creole English, aka Pidgin (Davis et al., 2005). Teachers further used comparative analyses of Standard English and Pidgin as a form of language learning that acknowledged students' primary language (Pidgin) while facilitating Standard English language development. By the end of the 3-year project, students who at first struggled to write a paragraph, wrote twelve to fifteen final term papers and developed corresponding public service announcements focused on social issues (e.g., bullying) that were broadcast on public television. Through these language practices, students developed a repertoire of language abilities that affirmed their multilingual identities and promoted academic achievement.

Our engaged ethnography as a transformative language policy processes approach further reflects and expands on community-based language and education advocacy through language practices that can inform effective instruction. We draw on García and Li's (2014) theories of language, languaging, and bilingualism that involve *"translanguaging* as a way to capture the fluid language practices of bilinguals without giving up the social construction of language and bilingualism under which speakers operate" (p. 5). García and Li use *bilingual education* as an umbrella term to encompass multilingual education in that it draws on all of minoritized students' home and community language resources. Thus, bilingual schools intend to affirm socially just practices and subsequently create more equitable educational opportunity. García, Zakharia, and Otcu (2013) more specifically describe bilingual education whereas three or more languages are used as media of instruction for oral communication and language/literacy learning. Teachers subsequently engage students' communities of language and literacy use through promoting translanguaging that draws on all of the students' language and literacy resources. García and Li (2014) suggest that

> ...what produces language as defined in school is the students' own creative languaging, drawing from their entire linguistic repertoire. Translanguaging in classrooms is an approach to bilingualism that is centered not on the acquisition and development of languages...but on the practices of bilingual students and their teachers that are readily observable and that are different from our traditional conceptions of autonomous languages.
>
> (p. 52)

In sum, we hold that restrictive language policies are the result of ideologies that intentionally or unintentionally impact human welfare. Our analyses are not just focused on language issues but on broader social welfare and equity challenges that are linked with language policies and practices. These analyses build on theories and practices of community-based dialogue and research that promote policies that acknowledge multilingualism and multiculturalism.

Engaged ethnography differs from and goes beyond other approaches in that it first and foremost takes a *critical reflexivity* stance that involves identifying and portraying the roles, responsibilities, knowledge, and actions of ethnographers (Clair, 2012). Critical reflexivity further reflects a postmodernist perspective that challenges the structuralist position of ethnographer detachment and displacement from critical social issues such as racial, linguistic, cultural, economic, political, and educational inequalities and discrimination generally. Marcus (1994) specifically argues that postmodern ethnographers continuously test the ground of equity conditions and, thus, realize "the strong engagement by authors with what goes on among particular subjects of study and of an equally strong reflexive engagement with their own self-making as scholars—in which qualitative social science is being remade" (p. 573). Thus, Marcus (1994) argues that conscious critical reflexivity should always be central to any and all forms of ethnography.

Reflexive engagement of another kind—one that focuses on participant ideological transformation—had already begun two decades earlier with Paulo Freire's landmark *Pedagogy of the Oppressed* that fostered ideological awareness among laborers. This approach, combined with activism, provides the means by which to achieve equitable social, economic, and educational equity. Mathers and Novelli (2007) argue that engaged ethnography

> ...challenges the conventional roles of relationships established by academics and generates new ones. The ethnographer does not stand outside the object of enquiry thereby adopting the role of "spectator," but stands alongside those engaged in struggle thereby taking the role of "witness" and even "active participant." In this sense, the ethnographer may find many paths to ethical and political commitment, but each of them involves him/her in undertaking a variety of acts of solidarity
> (p. 245)

Mathers and Novelli's (2007) position signaled a demarcation between ethnographic approaches that serve to report *outcomes* of research and an engaged approach that focuses on documenting the *processes* by which ideological awareness and social justice activism can occur. To clarify this distinction, we provide representative models of doing and reporting engagement that begin with Freire's pedagogy of the oppressed as a landmark consciousness-raising and liberatory approach. We then describe process-oriented models as represented by anthropologist Arjun Appadurai, social psychologists Michelle Fine and Monique Guishard, and emancipatory anthropologists David Gegeo and Karen Watson-Gegeo as they inform engaged ethnography and engaged language policy and practices.

Engaged Ethnography as Sociopolitical Practice

Paulo Freire's work arose from his long-term engagement in educational activities in Brazil that led him to challenge socioeconomic oppression through consciousness raising and ideological transformation among poor laborers.

His landmark theory of a dominant top-down "banking model of education" further led to development of a democratic form of learning in which students "come to see the world not as a static reality but as a reality in the process of transformation" (Macedo, 2000, p. 12). While Freire's (1970) work is well known and consequently often applied in research and practice, we specifically draw on his approach to re-envision ideological analyses that inform equitable language education policies and social change.

Freire (1970) defined "pedagogy of the oppressed" as the convergence of pain and hope; past and present; class struggles and liberation; we further argue that an engaged approach denounces current neoliberal and other dominant ideologies that create false hope for human progress through a free market economy. Freire's (1970) work also highlights the importance of researchers' own political position, or positionality, in research and praxis processes. In other words, given that oppression is socially constructed, Freire emphasizes the need for researchers' ideological clarity when intervening in the status quo. More specifically, he calls for denaturalization of ideological hegemony by critically examining how policies and institutional practices constitute oppression and disempower the disenfranchised. Macedo (2000) observes that Freire "teaches us with his penetrating and unquiet mind the meaning of a profound commitment to fight social injustice in our struggles to recapture the loss of our dignity as human beings" (p. 25). Harvey's (2005) analyses of social oppression further stresses the importance of interdisciplinarity in addressing inequality as shaped by the convergence of multiple factors such as class, ethnicity, race, language, education, and culture.

Freire and Macedo (2000) specifically denounce "neoliberal fatalism" in which "a minority makes most profits against the lives of the majority" and argues that not to resist this fatalistic position is to be part of "a perverse ethics" (p. 25–26). This process requires *conscientização,* that is, critical awareness of social, political, and economic contradictions as well as action against an oppressive reality. Such critical consciousness is not emotional; rather it is deeply rooted in concrete struggles of lower-middle-class laborers and other marginalized peoples who suffer under a social reality that fails to offer agency, power, and, thus, a sense of self-worth. Freire (1970, 1998) further argues that liberation is not possible by chance—rather, it is possible only through marginalized people's critical awareness of historical and ideological struggles and the "praxis of their quest" toward liberation. However, he stresses that the struggle against oppression is not easy. On the one hand, the power of dominant ideologies and practices is so deeply rooted in social structure that oppressed groups fear greater repression if they resist. On the other hand, they are denied space for developing critical awareness about social injustice given that state apparatuses, such as schools, reproduce dominant inequitable ideologies. Freire (1970) more specifically argues that "oppressive reality absorbs those within it and thereby acts to submerge human beings' consciousness" (p. 51). Thus, critical awareness for achieving liberation, the essence of the pedagogy of the oppressed, can be fostered only "*with*, not *for*, the oppressed in the incessant struggle to regain their humanity" (Freire, 1970, p. 48). Freire further holds that this liberatory process is not static but instead is made and remade according to evolving needs and sociopolitical conditions.

Freire (1970) further suggests that the participation of an engaged researcher-advocate is not necessarily immediately or at all welcomed. He argues that solidarity with the oppressed is the main component of the engaged process and can be achieved only by researcher demonstration of her or his sincere commitment to those who struggle for liberation in the face of power and domination. In other words, outsider engagement is possible only through empathy and solidarity with the oppressed and absolute commitment to transformation and liberation (see Mathers & Novelli, 2007). Yet we would argue that transformation and liberation best lie in the hands of the formerly and/or unconsciously oppressed. For example, Phyak's growing awareness of oppression as an indigenous Limbu community member and scholar most effectively and appropriately promotes liberation and decolonization of dominant ideologies at multiple levels and sites in Nepal.

While Freire (1970) provides two stages of engagement in the liberating process, Phyak (2016b) draws on ideological awareness to "unveil the world of oppression" and transform it through praxis. In other words, his goal is to help the disadvantaged come to understand how social injustice and marginalization are created and then explore ways in which this hegemony can be resisted. Phyak further draws on Freire's suggested second stage of the liberation process that attends to the degree to which people of all social classes are conscious of how they are oppressed or oppress. In other words, while the marginalized are engaged in unveiling ideological adversity that negatively impacts their sociopolitical, educational and economic well-being, there is also the need for the more privileged to become aware of ways in which they marginalize others (Davis & Phyak, 2015). Another case in point is the US *No Child Left Behind* situation in which teachers were helpless in resisting standardized curriculum and testing that potentially punishes rather than affirms marginalized students (also Brown, 2007). The movement toward tying teachers' performance, salary, and even their jobs to students' standardized test outcomes is also a form of oppression. Thus, the solution and outcomes of *collective* action in this situation attend to and yet go beyond Freire's *liberating pedagogy*. Engaged approaches that address public policies and institutional practices can potentially both embrace and surpass pedagogy of the oppressed to become pedagogy for collective and interactive liberation. For example, as teachers in the United States are forced to comply with state policies for curriculum and testing, both marginalized and middle-class students in public schools are likely disadvantaged by instruction that fails to socially and intellectually engage them. In a 2015 PBS Hawai'i–sponsored forum on education, the Hawai'i State Teacher's Association director stated "If Common Core Standards curriculum and (standardized) testing are so great, why doesn't Punahou (prestigious private K-12 school) buy into this?" The antidote for these marginalizing policies and practices is reflective dialogue.

Praxis—critical reflection on action—provides an important tool for engaging all participants in language policy discussion. It is through praxis that the marginalized understand policies and directives that "serve the interests of the oppressors whose image they have internalized" (Freire, 1970, p. 62). Mathers and Novelli (2007, p. 246) further argue that praxis "provides a rigorous and systematic approach to research that by grounding itself in everyday struggles can reveal important insights into resistance processes and develop new concepts and understandings that can inform better and more effective movement strategies." Drawing on their studies of resistance against privatization in Colombia and the *European Marches Network* against unemployment, job insecurity, and social exclusion in Europe, Mathers and Novelli (2007) claim that engaged ethnography as praxis "provides one possible route for critical academics not only to interpret the world but also to try and change it" (p. 246). Yet we go further by suggesting that those from a range of socioeconomic backgrounds can be challenged in their ability to gain awareness of their own personal and collective marginalization. As mentioned, public school educators in Hawai'i and across the United States experience negation of their professionalism through enforced use of standardized curriculum and testing. Teachers may consequently both experience oppression and oppress students through lack of critical consciousness and/or fear of losing their jobs. Until educators gain or regain awareness of ideologies and related policies that consequently suppress agency, they are likely to "accept their fate" (Freire, 1970, p. 64). A poignant case in point are the consequences of benign neglect of Pacific Islander school children whose families have left their homes due to rising ocean levels caused by global warming and ongoing illness resulting from radioactive fallout caused by nuclear testing on Bikini Island (Burkett, 2011). While also suffering the consequences of national policies, these displaced children in Hawai'i are denied effective multilingual education and are reportedly discriminated against and harassed (immigrant legal expert, personal communication). The Hawai'i Department of Education shows that nearly 50 percent of these students drop out of school every year.

In the foregoing and other cases of extreme discrimination, Freire (1970) states "dialogue with the people is radically necessary to every authentic revolution" (p. 128). He suggests that liberation is possible only through a pedagogy that acknowledges their sociopolitical struggles as resources for achieving freedom. He further asserts that dialogue cannot occur "between those who deny others the right to speak their word and those whose right to speak has been denied them" (Freire, 1970, p. 88). In order to have a meaningful dialogue, the communities we serve must have the opportunity to reclaim this right and subsequently prevent the continuation of dehumanizing aggression (Freire, 1970). Freire also holds that dialogue cannot exist without love, humility, trust, and hope for transformation. He further warns that "dialogue cannot be reduced to the act of one person's 'depositing' ideas in another, nor can it become a simple exchange of ideas to be "consumed" by the discussants. [...] It is an act of creation; it must not serve as a crafty instrument for the domination of one person by another" (Freire, 1970, p. 89). He further argues

> [A] true dialogue cannot exist unless the dialoguers engage in critical thinking—thinking which discerns an indivisible solidarity between the world and the people and admits of no dichotomy between them—thinking which perceives reality as process, as transformation, rather than as a static entity—thinking which does not separate itself from action, but constantly immerses itself in temporality without fear of the risks involved.
> (Freire, 1970, p. 92)

This speaks to the need for addressing current and future local, national, and global conditions of oppression. For example, while poverty continues and strife increases, what was legislated in Nepal as the rights of citizens to preserve their indigenous languages is now challenged by neoliberal actions, such as Nepal's promotion of English and Nepali in this highly linguistically and culturally diverse country. It is now unclear how politicians will cope with neoliberalism and other potentially devastating ideologies in the wake of the 2015 earthquakes and current neoliberal ideologies.

We hold that language policies and plans often fail when policy makers adopt a top-down "banking model" of education that serves elite interests while purposely ignoring the resources and challenges of those for whom the policies are directed. Second, policies such as NCLB and Common Core Standards in the United States were designed to disregard historical, cultural, economic, and sociopolitical conditions in which some groups are systematically dehumanized and denied the possibility of developing critical awareness. With situated adaptations, Freire's (1970) dialogic method can play an important role in engaging *all* language policy actors and recipients in critical exploration toward achieving ideological awareness and meaningful language, education, and social justice goals. As Macedo (2000) argues, dialogue should not be considered simply a method of engagement; rather it is a significant process of learning and knowing that invariably involves theorizing social critique.

Participatory Policy-making

While participatory action research and Freirian pedagogy of the oppressed models greatly inform much-needed situated consciousness raising, we further argue for an *engaged language policy and practices approach* that operates at the intersection of research and social justice action. As Fine (2009) suggests and we support, critical analysis is possible only when the most oppressed and disenfranchised are engaged in critical discussions concerning, in our case, language, education, and social justice. In the current neoliberal regime, oppressed and disenfranchised language policy actors are those most excluded from the decision-making process—teachers, parents, indigenous/immigrant communities, and youth. As demonstrated by Freirean and PAR approaches, action must first and foremost involve ideological consciousness raising among both the marginalized and marginalizing toward greater understanding of inequitable linguistic, social, and educational existential realities. This process involves collaboratively engaging in critical analysis of how current realities are connected with macro- and micro-level policies, social inequalities, historical oppression, and the enduring struggles of minoritized and indigenous populations.

In addition to Freire, we draw on other emancipatory models such as those of Appadurai, Fine, and Guishard toward further conceptualizing an engaged ethnographic and language policies and practices approach. Critical anthropologist Appadurai (2006) has developed and portrayed active engagement with socioeconomic policies and practices through his on-the-ground critical work with college students in Mumbai, India. Students explore, construct, and perform both local and global knowledge through ideological analyses and participatory research. For example, through his nongovernmental organization Partners for Urban Knowledge Action and Research (PUKAR) project in Mumbai, India, Appadurai (2006) portrays how youth engage in exploring multiple issues, meanings, and images of the city in which they live. Through grassroots activism projects, he engages young people from a variety of fields (e.g., architects, journalists, teachers, sociologists) in developing action plans for improved living conditions and services. In the Neighborhood Project, youth explored and documented urban "existential realities" through essays, photographs, and film representing the challenges of inadequate housing and living conditions. Thus, they subsequently engaged in critical dialogue concerning local challenges toward envisioning situated possibilities. A vision for transformation through critical analysis and liberation from poverty allowed youth to "speak up as active citizens" about the issues affecting their lives and community. By doing this, youth obtain "full citizenship" in both acknowledging local and global challenges and realizing possibilities for positive change (Appadurai, 2006). Appadurai further argues for the "right to research" to promote equal distribution of global knowledge and knowledge of globalization, both necessary components for world citizenship and strong democracies.

Gegeo and Watson-Gegeo's (2002) early landmark ethnographic work in the Solomon Islands acknowledged the need for engagement with local people toward resisting Western colonial and capitalist ideologies of development, knowledge, and education. They suggest that engagement is a form of social critique through which the researchers and villagers collaboratively explore issues of poverty, suffering, and ethnic tensions while also identifying the hegemony of colonial ideologies that impact community development and education. Anthropologists Low and Merry (2010) support this approach in suggesting that the engaged researcher should critique the "misuse of concepts within everyday discourse, particularly when these concepts lead to discriminatory behaviors" (p. 208). Gegeo and Watson-Gegeo (2002, 2013) further promote local indigenous epistemology for sustainable development by first critically analyzing how colonial ideologies "unrecognized" the importance of traditional knowledge and skills in development initiatives. They critique the ways in which contemporary emphasis on globalization, global capitalism, economic restructuring, and free trade has intensified pressure on fragile economies like that of the Solomon Islands to focus on large-scale, centralized, export industries. They further argue that such an emphasis "continues to ignore political, educational, and humanistic aspects, rural needs, and the importance of traditional cultures and their significance to national development" (p. 378). In work with Kwara'ae youth and villagers, Gegeo and Watson-Gegeo engaged in narrating counter-discourse positions in response to increasing imposition of foreign knowledge and development. They most recently worked with villagers toward community-based development initiatives based on indigenous epistemologies. This engagement was guided by indigenous critical praxis in which villagers engaged in "critical reflection on culture, history, knowledge, politics, economics, and the sociopolitical contexts in which people themselves are living their lives; and then take the next step of acting on these critical reflections" (Gegeo & Watson-Gegeo, 2013, p. 399). Gegeo and Watson-Gegeo (2013) more specifically attended village meetings, participated in local youth clubs/activities, and closely observed local/global ideological and epistemological tensions within the community. This engagement constituted a transformative process by which Gegeo and Watson-Gegeo ensured participation, voice, and epistemologies of the local people. Thus, Gegeo and Watson-Gegeo's (2013) work renders ethnography an "anti-hegemonic science" (Blommaert, 2009, p. 258) and "science of activism and intervention" (Luke, 1996, p. vii).

As a whole, these and other representations of activism and intervention subsequently have the ability to inform *engaged language policy and practices* toward models of social justice action that bring about societal equity transformation. Toward this end, we suggest the need for identifying and modeling community-based reform and localized language education policies.

Toward Community-Based Research and Reform

We argue that while engaged ethnographic approaches to language education policy design and planning can be effective, there have been few reports on the processes by which local language policy change take place. The *Community*

Organizing and School Reform Project designed by Harvard University activist professors Mark R. Warren and Karen L. Mapp and their graduate students (2011) provides documentation of community organizing as catalysts for school reform. They state

> ...we understand community as a historically shaped and emergent phenomenon, not a static one. Organizing groups become an active agent in this historic and ongoing process, providing a vehicle for people to build the capacity of their community. From this point of view, we can better understand that community organizing is not about applying a set of techniques to mobilize individuals. Strong organizing groups dig into and emerge out of a community's historical tradition...They help craft a new chapter in a community's story as they expand and reorganize relationships while people work to put into practice dynamic understandings of their deeply held values.
>
> (Warren & Mapp, 2011, p. 21)

While ethnographers have long engaged in sociocultural studies of language socialization (Ochs & Schieffelin, 2009), development, and situated use within and beyond communities, we emphasize the need for understanding the nature of language policy research and its potentially positive impact when conducted with rather than on communities. Phyak (2016b) engages Limbu indigenous villagers in ethnographic observation of language policies and practices in school, community, and home, first, and then involves them in critical dialogue on what they have observed and experienced in the community. This dialogue provides villagers with opportunities to interrogate their own ideologies of language and education toward awareness of how they are affected by dominant language and political discourses, ideologies and policies. Initial dialogue revealed that indigenous villagers reproduce an ideology of English as a "modern" and "educated people's" language while viewing Nepali as the "national language." In further reflecting on language practices and policies in local schools and communities, villagers found that indigenous languages are continually displaced because of English and Nepali language dominance. For example, one villager, whose two children go to a local secondary school, replied to the question of indigenous Limbu language use as follows:

> It's hard to say...but Limbu isn't widely used in the community. Young people don't speak Limbu at home. I think it is because they don't use it in school. Schools don't teach Limbu. Parbate [Nepali] is sarkari [official/ government] language. Angreji [English] is famous now. Boarding schools teach in English. These schools are expensive. Rich people send their children to private school. So we have two types of education...

for rich people and the poor people. Parents think that their children become smarter when they speak English. It's called a modern language and the language of civilized people. So schools focus on teaching English and Nepali. People think that *Aani Paan* [our language] has no use in education. People think that *Aani Paan* has no relevance outside. All have this kind of thinking.

These views reveal both ideological hegemony of English-Nepali bilingualism and the frustration of villagers toward the current language policy discourses and practices. As they engage in further dialogue, the villagers reveal ideological tensions with regard to the use of Limbu in school and other public spheres. The villager/researcher cited earlier emphasizes that "*Aani Paan* is important. It's our identity. But we're powerless. We aren't aware. We don't make policies. Until now we don't have power to make policies, we should accept other's policies."

The engaged, liberatory, and participatory forms of research described here reflect the need for moving from conducting *research on others* toward *shared inquiry with others*. In the following chapters, we expand on the range and purposes of engaged inquiry with villagers, teachers, students, parents, administrators and all involved others in developing collective ideological awareness, resisting unjust language policies and practices, and sharing local and global knowledge.

4

PLANNING RESISTANCE AND DISCOVERING ALTERNATIVES

Canagarajah's (1999) *Resisting Linguistic Imperialism in English Language Teaching* has received ongoing attention among those concerned with resisting global English language policies. Ranging from language rights movements to growing interest in multilingual education, scholars have increasingly countered language policies that deny minoritized languages and multilingual practices in the public sphere (May, 2008, 2012; Ricento, 2006; Tupas, 2015). These and other scholars (Lin, 2013; Tollefson, 2013) argue for resisting hegemonic nation-state and neoliberal ideologies toward promoting equitable language policies and practices. Lin (2013) suggests that

> [W]e....need to confront ourselves with a central set of tasks or questions: why are students and teachers constantly put under such language policies that are counterproductive to their learning and teaching? What are the legitimation processes of such policies, and what (are) the hegemonic mechanisms at work? Why are these hegemonies so persistent and difficult to break? What can initiate change in language policy and planning? What further resources can local actors harness to counter the hegemony of these policies?
>
> (p. 224)

Critical language policy researchers are increasingly examining the impact of national policies on multilingual learners and subsequently have argued for multilingual policies that support the use of students' home languages in public spheres. Manan, David, and Dumanig (2016) have drawn on the Foucauldian (1991) theory of "governmentality" to analyze the purposes for and means by which schools in Pakistan suppress the use of local indigenous languages. Their analysis suggests that while Urdu and English are being promoted in schools, indigenous languages are marginalized as a result of hegemonic neoliberal language commodification. While emphasizing the need for resisting inequitable privileging of languages in education, Manan et al. (2016) further argue for "…a comprehensive paradigmatic shift in favor of additive multilingual policies in education" (p. 19). Malsbary and Appelgate (2016) explore the challenges of meeting US immigrant English language learners' needs in an environment of high-stakes testing policies that focus on student output while ignoring teacher challenges in providing effective instruction. The authors also note the school emphasis on what students are lacking (English) rather than honoring the emerging bilingual/bicultural assets of students. Alimi (2016) critiques the dominance of English-Setswana bilingualism in Botswana public domains while acknowledging that community-based advocacy contributes to creating space for minoritized languages. While indigenous languages are restricted to local or tribal communication, Alimi calls for a cultural reawakening through community activities toward altering the English/Setswana linguistic landscape in favor of multilingualism/multiculturalism as an inherent characteristic of the country. These scholars speak to the need for planning resistance to inequitable and/or inadequate language policies at the national, regional, and local levels.

We hold that ideological, critical, and emancipatory processes are necessary for comprehensive remediation of marginalizing policies. With the increasing influx of cross-national migrants and corresponding language diversity, we need an alternative policy approach for families struggling to maintain their linguistic heritage while accommodating new languages and cultures. Migrants and local/ indigenous residents are currently caught up in ideologies that may include one- nation-one-language policies; multilingualism that favors middle and upper classes; and/or a rigid language education policy that fails to meet the needs of linguistically diverse populations, including speakers of minoritized language varieties. While portraying ways in which engaged efforts are situated in historical as well as evolving social, cultural, and political circumstances at specific sites is important, we argue for ideological transformation toward the right to participate in language policy processes (Ramanathan, 2013). For example, although English will undoubtedly remain the lingua franca of the United States, past and current bilingual education programs reveal that it is possible and desirable to maintain the home language for effective content learning while learning English through bilingual/multilingual schooling (Baker, 2011; Cummins, 2006). We further argue here for moving beyond descriptive accounts of injustice and toward portrayals of activist efforts that inform and support egalitarian language policy and planning on the ground. Thus, we hold that while descriptions of language policies, planning, and action are important, they often fail to realize ideological awareness that would help to articulate viable solutions to inequity and achieve effective equitable language policy transformation.

Planning Resistance

Once marginalizing and ineffective national, state, and regional language ideologies and policies are uncovered, they require addressing through determining effective, equitable, and theoretically informed resistance. We draw here on our previous call for ideological analyses that inform the politics of local, national, and global policies; the processes involved in establishing equitable policies; and portrayal of these processes toward models of equitable and effective language policies and plans. While researchers such as Harvey (2005) and Lipman (2011) explore the impact of neoliberal ideologies of unregulated market and privatization on public services such as education, a number of scholars are calling for on-the-ground language policies that resist, negotiate, and appropriate inequitable policies (Davis, 2009; McGroarty, 2006, 2013; Tollefson, 2013; Wyman, McCarty, & Nicholas, 2014). We portray here our own language policy work in Nepal and Hawai'i, respectively, toward models of resistance to and alternatives for discriminatory policies. Phyak focuses on engaged language policy efforts with indigenous youth and villagers in Nepal, while Davis draws on her activist collaboration with schools and communities in Hawai'i toward promoting minoritized languages and multilingual policies in education.

The engaged language policy processes we discuss here critically look at the importance of local resistance to monolingual ideologies in multilingual nations. We emphasize the ways in which different actors take an agentive role in challenging and transforming language policies that affect their educational and sociopolitical lived experiences. While keeping ideological analyses at the center, we explore alternative ideologies that support the space for students' linguistic and cultural knowledge. In other words, engaged language policy, as discussed in this chapter, pays attention to the means by which different language policy actors develop ideological awareness towards denaturalizing dominant ideologies. The examples we discuss are informed by the theories and practices of collaborative inquiry, community engagement and situated language policies.

Our engaged approach places all concerned participants at the center of exploration and liberating transformation (Cammarota & Fine, 2008; hooks, 1994) and promotes the means by which the dispossessed work to possess the right to research, advocate, and acquire sustainable, equitable, and self-defined honorable ways of learning and living (Appadurai, 2006; Gegeo & Watson-Gegeo, 2013). An inquiry approach also draws on critical and participatory research methods in documenting ways in which the disenfranchised negotiate multiple identities and roles to help to disrupt hegemonic policies, ideologies, and practices (Giampapa & Lamoureux, 2011; Patiño Santos, 2011). We specifically utilize Fine's (2006) ethnographic *democratic engagement* approach in which the researcher and participants work collaboratively toward collective empowerment. Our engaged ethnography centrally documents alternative ways in which indigenous/immigrant/migrant youth, teachers, educators, and community members collectively adapt, resist, and transform harmful ideologies and policies. We specifically take up Appadurai's (2006) call for helping young people to achieve full citizenship in a global society through making strategic inquiries and gaining strategic knowledge in areas such as educational disparities, transmigration challenges, and global/local crises. Thus, we address language issues that are closely aligned with neoliberal actions that essentially commodify social disparity.

We take the position that in marketing English and Western education ideologies and epistemologies, state and for-profit/non-profit organizations are essentially marketing social reproduction (Bourdieu, 1991; Phillipson, 2012). In other words, those who have the least access to social commodities such as geographic (urban), higher social class, multilingual, and technological resources are least likely to succeed in the English/Western education market place (see Kirkpatrick, 2013; Luke, 2011). At the same time, the promise if not the actuality of socioeconomic benefit from English language learning can nonetheless pose threats to indigenous languages, home/heritage languages, and, more generally, multilingualism/multiculturalism that could otherwise provide alternative epistemologies for addressing pressing social needs (Lin, 2013; Skutnabb-Kangas & Heugh, 2012). Thus, we have argued for an engaged language policy and practices approach that includes and goes beyond language in engaging human welfare challenges such as poverty, dislocation, global warming, armed conflict, crime, and health issues (Davis, 2014). Intersecting sociodiversity and biodiversity crises are also addressed by activist-scholars such as Martinez-Alier (2002) who argues for an environmentalism of the poor that reveals and counters the inequitable impact of economic colonialism, imperialism, and globalization. Thus, issues of social and safety concern, regard for environmental impact, and countering harmful Western neoliberal/assimilationist intent suggest the need for critical awareness and action that address language policies and local education concerns. Activism further strives toward awakening a sense of injustice not only among the oppressed, but with those who possess material and cultural power.

We further emphasize that engaged ethnography and language policy/practices intersect through "a meeting of multiple sides in an encounter with and among others, one in which there is negotiation and dialogue toward substantial and viable meanings that make a difference" (Madison, 2012, p. 10). We specifically argue for grounding collective analyses in awareness of macro-level ideologies and imposed policies/practices that are detrimental to human and educational welfare. In promoting awareness, we emphasize the need for researchers/community facilitators to take seriously their position as learner and advocate in dialogue with key participants in the engaged process. We have suggested placing all those directly involved at the center of emancipatory processes. Thus, rather than describing research outcomes, ELP aims to *portray* ways in which all concerned individuals and institutions—policy makers, administrators, teachers, parents/community members, students, schools, local organizations—are joined in processes of developing awareness of inequitable ideologies as well as the means by which to challenge inhumane, demeaning, and exclusionary policies and practices from within. We also focus on documentation of processes involved in challenging neoliberal and inequitable top-down policy-making. We further suggest the need for *portraying dialogic processes of growing collective awareness* of local, national, and global neoliberal conditions toward transforming inequitable policies and practices. We specifically advocate reflective positionality and long-term engagement through which ethnographers/engaged others facilitate inclusive participant involvement toward linguistic and social equity.

While engaged ethnography calls for an intimate understanding of policies and politics at multiple sites, it also demands engaged actions toward changing inequitable situations. With this in mind, we draw on our own work and other recent models of documentation and emancipation that portray how ideological analyses with communities, educators, researchers, and concerned others can raise awareness of harmful neoliberal commodification and standardization of language education policies (Block, Gray, & Holborow, 2012; Luke, Luke, & Graham, 2007). We specifically draw on ways in which local participants, forward-looking activists/advocates engage in collective plans for resisting marginalizing and ineffective national, state, and/or regional language ideologies and policies. These efforts are intended to aid in developing and documenting language and education policies that are locally relevant and educationally forward-looking and serve to provide models for wider change. Documenting processes further suggests reporting development of instructional practices that support teachers in building on local knowledge toward schooling that is relevant and engaging for all students.

We also employ our advocacy work in Nepal and Hawai'i toward illustrating engaged policy and planning that attends to linguistic and social equity. Having been born and raised in a multilingual and multiethnic Limbu community in Nepal, Phyak has an intimate understanding of the politics and possibilities of language policies and practices in his home country. Davis's 20 years of language education advocacy in Hawai'i allows for insight into the situated diversity challenges as well as possibilities in this US state. Thus, we provide these models of our advocacy work in Nepal and Hawai'i toward articulating ideological becoming and the potential for on-the-ground policy transformation.

Ideological Transformation in Nepal

An ideology of inequality is deeply rooted in Nepal's history of a hierarchical class and caste system involving ethnicity, gender, social, and economic positioning. A number of Nepali scholars (e.g., Gurung, 2006; Hachchethu, 2003; Pandey, 2012) are critical of the nation-state's policies and political systems in which indigenous ethnic minorities, women, and those from rural areas are excluded or underrepresented in the political system. Lawoti (2010) and Hangen (2010) specifically criticize the high caste (traditionally Bahun-Chetri) monopoly over the policy-making process (also see Das & Hatlebakk, 2010) that contributes to increasing underrepresentation of minoritized people in state mechanisms and to abandonment of indigenous languages and cultures. Phyak (2011) argues that this historical caste and class system inevitably contributed to recent language education policies and practices.

Phyak (2016a) suggests that the adoption of a neoliberal free market ideology in the 1990s paved the way for foreign investment and privatization of public services. He critiques Nepal's plans for infrastructure development as well as socioeconomic and educational reforms guided by a global neoliberal economic ideology (Shakya, 2009) that challenges local socioeconomic equality and civil rights. Phyak further draws on Pandey (2012) to explain how Nepal's dependence on foreign aid further contributes to "failed development" in describing a recent United Nations Development Program report that shows that Nepal falls within the category of "least developed" countries (UNDP, 2014). At the same time, this report argues, socioeconomic and educational disparity between the rich and the poor is widening. The 2010–2011 National Living Standards Survey (Central Bureau of Statistics, 2011) shows that more than 47 percent of the country's production of goods is consumed by the richest 20 percent while the poorest 20 percent consume only 8 percent.

Since the country relies heavily on funding from international donor agencies such as the World Bank and Asian Development Bank, Phyak suggests how both explicit and implicit education policies further serve the strategic interests of donors. With foreign investment in educational projects such as the *School Sector Reform Program* and *Higher Education Project*, public/private schools and higher education are in the process of moving away from national administration toward neoliberal management (Regmi, 2016). The World Bank's heavily funded education reform projects embody neoliberalism through promoting so-called "effective schooling" as determined through promotion of English and corresponding quantified scores on achievement tests (see Carney, 2003). This increasingly common tactic of setting up economic dependency through neoliberal colonization ignores the sociopolitical, economic, and linguistic challenges of Nepal and the central need for national and local agency. Thus, while an increasing gap in quality schooling is being created between the rich and the poor, valuable indigenous language and cultural resources as well as the potential for effective bilingual/multilingual education are being lost.

As part of our ELP approach, Phyak has observed and conducted critical analyses with youth and villagers on the increasing dominance of Western economic ideologies underlying educational, environmental, and socioeconomic policies and practices. More specifically, he works with indigenous people in exploring and analyzing how neoliberalism has created challenges for local languages in education and other public spheres.

Phyak engages indigenous youth and villagers in exploring and resisting hegemonic ideologies that affect their lived educational and sociopolitical experiences. Through engaging in critical dialogue, youth and villagers analyze how language issues intersect with broader sociopolitical ideologies. Given the state's national policies are deeply influenced by neoliberal ideologies, educational reform has embraced privatization and market-based competition by determining the quality of education (Regmi, 2016). Phyak's dialogic engagement with indigenous youth and villagers specifically reveals the means by which neoliberal ideologies in education have reproduced socioeconomic and educational inequalities. For example, one villager contends that "private schools are expensive[...]. Poor people cannot send their children to private schools. ...We have now two types of schools. Private schools are for the rich people and public schools are for the poor." One youth further observed that "students from private schools are considered smart because they speak English." However, as the villagers and youth continue to engage in dialogue they become critically aware of how neoliberal ideologies of private and competitive education exacerbate unequal power relations between the rich and the poor. For example, in critically reflecting on current educational policies, one youth asserts that "two education systems have produced two groups of students. Private-school students are successful in national exams because they get extra support from both parents and schools. But public school students fail in national exams because they do not receive much educational support. The government has to think about improving public education. Public-school students cannot even go to college as they fail in school level national exams."

As the youth and villagers engage in dialogue, they also become aware of the conditions of their own linguistic and cultural marginalization. They are particularly critical about how the state is not taking a proactive approach towards supporting language minoritized children. One villager, for example, contends that "the state is now focusing on English, but not on local languages... not on mother tongues." While dominant policies and practices continue to reproduce neoliberal ideologies of language competence through quantitative test scores (Carney, 2003), dialogic engagement with youth and villagers further show that such test scores do not necessarily reflect the sociopolitical, linguistic, and cultural struggles of ethnic minoritized students in public schools.

The critical issue that emerges in Phyak's engaged work with villagers and indigenous youth is the question of access and representation of indigenous ethnic minorities in policy-making and planning. Phyak and collaborating youth and villagers realized as early as 2010 the need for substantive critical and strategic engagement of both villagers and youth leading to resistance, negotiation, and transformation of hegemonic and monolingual ideologies.

Phyak has subsequently engaged Limbu indigenous villagers in ethnographic observation of language policies and practices in schools, communities, and homes. Villagers then collectively and critically reflect on what they have observed and experienced in the community toward gaining ideological awareness. Thus, critical ethnography provides villagers with the means by which to gain awareness of how their lives are affected by dominant language and political discourses. The government supported the discourse of English as a "modern" and "educated people's" language, and promotion of the elite Nepali language has increasingly displaced indigenous languages. As illustrated in the previous chapter, a village elder holds that "*Aani Paan* (our language) is important. It's our identity. But we're powerless. We aren't aware. We don't make policies. Until we have power to make policies, we must accept other's policies." These views show both the ideological hegemony of English-Nepali bilingualism and the frustration and helplessness of villagers facing neoliberal language policy discourse and practices. As they engage in further dialogue, the villagers reveal increasing ideological tension with regard to the possibilities of using the indigenous Limbu language in school and other public spheres.

Discovering Alternatives: Critical Dialogue in Nepal

Critical dialogue has promoted villagers' understanding of counter-histories and counter-narratives about language, identity, education, and nationalism. Phyak's roles in this process have involved contributing to discussions as a member of the Limbu community, providing additional information from academic studies, and posing questions toward continuing critical and productive dialogue. In a series of discussions, Phyak suggested ways in which multilingual education policy is necessary for Limbu children. The villagers agreed that the use of Limbu in schools helps their children understand and maintain their culture and history while more effectively participating in the learning process. While engaging in dialogue concerning the costs and benefits of various language policies, the villagers became increasingly critical of the state ideology of language policy that discriminates explicitly and implicitly against indigenous people. For example, in commenting on the historical and contemporary oppression of indigenous language due to the state's linguistic nationalism and neoliberal ideologies, one villager recounts the following:

> The state's one-nation-one-language policy has given power to Nepali native speakers. These days Limbu children also speak good Nepali. But they don't get chance to use Limbu in school. In our time, Limbu was legally banned in school and in government offices. Now people talk about mother tongue education. Our school also taught Limbu for a couple of years. But it is stopped now. We don't have Limbu language teachers and textbooks. The government doesn't give equal priority to our language. Nepali and English are given more emphasis from the first grade. In practice, Nepali is still considered a national language. And English has been a fashion these days. Public schools in this village have started introducing English as medium of instruction policy. They've begun to compete with private schools. Student number is going down in public schools because of private schools in the village.

Yet, while the government earlier developed a mother tongue–based multilingual education policy, the recent ideological construction of Nepali as a national language and English as a central language in the global neoliberal market place has posed serious challenges for creating space for indigenous languages in schools (Phyak, 2013). Thus, indigenous language education and thereby local multilingualism is framed as a problem rather than a linguistic and epistemological resource (Blackledge & Creese, 2010; Creese & Blackledge, 2010; Weber & Horner, 2012). When asked why public schools are placed in the position of competing with private schools that offer English medium education, a headmaster of a school, who was a participant in dialogue with the villagers, revealed that "private schools are established in the village. They advertise English medium of instruction as their selling point to attract parents and students." Clearly, ideologies of multilingualism in Nepal and elsewhere face formidable obstacles in attempts to counter historically established and neoliberally sold educational policies and practices.

Engaged Resistance to Nepali National Policies

While recognizing the challenges involved in resisting, negotiating, and transforming dominant neoliberal ideologies, a number of scholars (e.g., Davis, 2009b; McCarty, 2014; Menken, 2013; Shohamy, 2006) have shown that policies can be changed through raising critical awareness at intersecting micro- (community), meso- (school), and macro- (nation-state) levels. The engagement of villagers in ethnographic observation of language policies and practices through co-constructed dialogue on relevant sociopolitical issues have been effective ways in which to raise ideological awareness among indigenous peoples toward resisting dominant language ideologies.

Phyak further builds on participatory models of youth (Appadurai, 2006; Wyman, McCarty, & Nicholas, 2014) and villagers (Gegeo & Watson-Gegeo,

2001, 2013) as transformative agents who portray resistance to covert and overt language policies in the face of neoliberal adversity. In assuming a collaborative co-learning approach (see Li, 2014), Phyak works closely with Limbu youth who are members of the *Limbu Students' Forum*, in exploring and addressing the sociopolitical, linguistic, economic, and educational challenges of indigenous peoples. These youth promote villager policy engagement through ethnographic exploration of language and cultural practices in communities and schools and by organizing a series of workshops at local and national levels. The workshops include youth focus group discussion as well as *dialogue* and *critical praxis* with teachers, students, and parents toward strengthening their own and others' critical awareness of dominant language ideologies, policies, and practices. Phyak and youth further link on-the-ground language practices with ideologies underlying macro-policies and sociopolitical practices. For example, one youth portrayed a local head teacher's views on English as a medium of instruction from the first grade onward as follows:

> I'm surprised to know that schools are not serious about language issue. Sir's [headmaster's] views show that English is like everything. He said "learning English is like achieving quality education. That's why the school adopted an English medium policy." But it isn't good. If we think that education in English is the best education, then local languages will disappear. It's important to learn English, but local languages are equally important for children. If schools don't use local languages then children don't see value of using their own home languages. This is happening now. I don't believe that students learn effectively in English. It's hard for them to understand English …Teachers also don't speak English fluently…How can students achieve 'quality education'? I think it's just a mentality.

As youth analyzed dominant language ideologies as reproduced by teachers and schools, they became increasingly critical of the linkage of English with "quality education." More specifically, they came to view the rationalization of English as the medium of instruction for quality education as "just a mentality" rather than a reality. Youth further challenged the ideological hegemony of English and promoted the personal and academic value of local languages in communities and schools. Although these youth acknowledge the possible advantages of learning English in school, they are critical of its use as the sole medium of instruction.

Youth are further engaged in analyzing how the displacement of local languages and the increased ideological hegemony of English are linked with the broader sociopolitical ideology of the state. The youth engaged in analyses of how the privatization of education has supported an English language policy, which eventually forced public schools to adopt an English medium of education policy in villages. Youth further came to realize that privatization of education has contributed to division of citizens into two groups, the rich and the poor. For example, in commenting on the impact of private schools in shaping villager language ideologies, one youth stated,

> I agree with what [local public school] teacher said. Private schools focus on teaching in English. Most aware and rich parents send their children to private school. They can give extra care for their education. They let their children study at home. So private school students do better. But public school students have to help their parents…they've got to work in the field and do household work. Most parents aren't educated. These parents think that private schools are better than public schools. They also want to send their children to private schools…they want their children to speak English. Most parents don't know about the importance of using local languages in school. So they accept what schools teach. Parents are very much influenced by private schools. As private schools don't use local languages, parents think that the use of local languages isn't relevant in education. The government has to think about this. It has to make policies that support local languages in both private and public schools.

This youth articulates national movement toward privatization and a Western neoliberal ideology of education (Harvey, 2005) that deeply affects the language and schooling ideologies of the common people.

Phyak further worked with youth to organize and facilitate a series of workshops on language policy and multilingualism in education at national and local levels. The goals were to engage youth in further dialogue on language policy issues and develop plans for action to create space for indigenous languages in education. We describe here a 10-hour *Language Policy and Youth* workshop that was organized in July 2014 with indigenous youth studying in one of the constituent campuses of Tribhuvan University in eastern Nepal. Thirty-three students representing various ethnic and caste groups were present at the workshop. The discussion began with a brief overview of the global and local linguistic situation and led up to exploring the national mother tongue-based multilingual education policy that allows for indigenous medium of instruction in schools up to grade 3 (Hough, Thapa-Magar, & Yonjan-Tamang, 2009; Phyak, 2011, 2013; Rai, Rai, Phyak, & Rai, 2011). The participants discussed both macro-policies and micro-realities in groups. Participants then formed groups to discuss the sociolinguistic situation of their own community; the reasons why children stop using their mother tongue; and the importance of using indigenous languages in education. Each group came up with a visual interpretation of the Nepali situation of language policy (Figure 4.1).

In this figure, one group provides a pastoral representation of Nepal's ideological situation. They explained:

Planning Resistance and Discovering Alternatives **69**

FIGURE 4.1 An indigenous youth ideological map of Nepal

> The blindfolded man at one end of the bridge represents the common people, particularly ethnic minorities, who are not informed about the policies. Although there are policies that allow the use of indigenous languages in education, ethnic minorities are already blind-folded. ... They are in the darkness. They don't know where to go. They aren't sure what languages should be used in school. Without being aware of the importance of multilingual and indigenous languages, they cannot take strong activist positions. ... You know ... they might fall into the river.

The workshop participants revealed increasing critical awareness of the discriminatory nature of current policies and educational practices. They drew on visual representations to further articulate increasing understanding of the sociopolitical situation. For example, one participant suggested that "the blindfolded man at one end of the bridge represents the ethnic minoritized people who are not able to resist discriminatory language policies. We [ethnic minorities] take dominant language practices for granted." She further suggested an increasing awareness of collusion in their own oppression by stating, "We ran after Nepali-only policy and now we are running after the English language fashion. We are bound to do so because we cannot go across the bridge (to critical awareness)."

In the next stage, these youth make their own plans to raise awareness of parents and other youth about the significance of multilingualism to create space for indigenous languages in education in their respective communities.

In each of four groups, youth developed their own activist plans and activities. Some of the major activities are as follows:

- Carry out a feasibility study for introducing indigenous languages in local schools: Go to the community and observe the language situation. After that talk to the parents and teachers about the possibility of multilingual education.
- Organize awareness-raising activities in the community and school: Discuss the importance of multilingualism and indigenous languages in education with parents, students, political leaders, and teachers.
- Collaborate with stakeholders, social organizations, schools, and other institutions to promote multilingualism and the use of indigenous languages in school.
- Generate funding from various resources such as the Village Development Committee, District Education Office, and other organizations.
- Collect indigenous funds of knowledge (e.g., weaving skills and herbal medicine) and cultural practices, and develop resources materials by using them. Work with teachers to use the materials for instructional purposes.
- Monitor whether schools actually use indigenous languages in classrooms.

Through engagement in language policy dialogue, the youth challenge both linguistic nationalism and neoliberal ideologies of language policy. As they become aware of marginalizing ideologies, they develop a strong sense of agency and activism toward claiming their role as advocates for indigenous languages and multilingual education. Following the foregoing plans, youth have organized discussions with villagers in their native languages on language policies along with indigenous languages and history. Youth have further collaborated with local teachers and schools/colleges to replace bilingual (English-Nepali) billboards with multilingual (English-Nepali-Limbu) ones. Reflecting on their activist work, one youth argues,

> The state doesn't do anything to support indigenous language at the local level. It just says that the indigenous peoples have right to use their languages. But it doesn't help in practice. People aren't aware. The state should take responsibility to promote local languages in school. Policy isn't enough. The state should take all languages (as) equal. Linguistic and cultural diversity is our asset.

The youth claim activist identities through this critical praxis approach. The ideological awareness they developed through ethnographic exploration of language policies and practices as well as in critical dialogue strengthen their commitment toward promoting linguistic and cultural diversity in education.

Their plans and related actions are reflective of growing ideological awareness about ongoing discourses, ideologies, and language policy practices.

Phyak's engaged work with indigenous youth and villagers supports Linda Smith's (2012) theories and practices regarding "decolonizing" ideologies. While engaging in collaborative dialogue built on critical ethnographic exploration of language policies and practices, youth and villagers not only challenge dominant language ideologies but promote an alternative ideology that supports the use of local multilingualism in education. Phyak's engaged work also supports Appadurai's (2006) "right to research" and Gegeo and Watson-Gegeo's (2001, p. 203) "critical villagers" as transformative agents to portray how indigenous participants engage covert and overt language policies in the face of neoliberal adversity. In building a collaborative co-learning approach (Li, 2014), Phyak's work with youth and villagers provides critical insights into understanding how engaged ethnography can be a method for addressing the sociopolitical, linguistic, economic, and educational challenges of indigenous peoples and rural villagers. As the youth and villager develop critical consciousness through dialogue, they take a strong activist position to promoting indigenous languages in education.

Engaging in Neoliberal Resistance in Hawai'i

Central to addressing inequality in Hawai'i is the need to uncover and portray an ideology of language and ethnic discrimination that arose and is maintained through a history of colonization and shifting ethnic hierarchies. Prior to the first arrival of Europeans in 1778, the inhabitants of the Hawaiian Islands had developed a highly organized social system, a recognized Polynesian language that became known as Hawaiian, and established a constitutional government. Yet, Hawaiian governance as well as language and cultural practices were increasingly threatened through US missionary settlement and sugar plantation development. While the Hawaiian nation struggled for continued independence, linguistic and cultural autonomy was further threatened when in 1851 plantation owners began recruiting migrant labor from China, Russia, Germany, Portugal, Norway, Japan, Korea, and the Philippines and instituted a contract labor system that was essentially indentured servitude. Linguistic diversity served to counter organizing against unfair labor conditions and, in efforts to further discourage indigenous governance by the Republic of Hawai'i, the state banned the Hawaiian language in all public and private schools in 1896. However, with the help of Pidgin (which evolved into Hawai'i Creole English) as a growing lingua franca among plantation workers and Hawaiians, in 1946 the International Longshore and Warehouse Union brought linguistic and cultural groups together in a strike that lasted 79 days and successfully shut down the sugar industry (Kent, 2004). While labor conditions subsequently improved, at the same time, the State legislature began lobbying for US statehood, primarily to avoid US tariffs on sugar. With objections from Hawaiians loyal to the monarchy and from legislators on the mainland who felt its majority non-white population "inappropriate" for an American state, *The Act to Provide for the Admission of the State of Hawai'i into the Union* (Pub.L. 86–3, March 18, 1959) was nonetheless enacted by the United States Congress and signed into law by President Dwight D. Eisenhower.

The post-statehood Americanization era saw the banning of the Hawaiian language, suppression of a multilingual press, closure of heritage language schools, and ongoing attempts to eradicate Hawai'i Creole English (Pidgin) in public schools through creation of English Standard schools. The Standard schools subsequently led to private institutions which now serve the majority of upper- and middle-class students, thus representing the highest percentage of private school enrollment in the United States (Poythress, 2010). Yet in the face of this Standard English language stance, activist Hawaiians took to the streets to protest the ban on their language and subsequently won recognition in 1978 of Hawaiian as an official state language that has equal status with English. In 1986, Hawaiians and supporters battled and won against the law banning Hawaiian-medium instruction in public schools. The Ka Papahana Kaiapuni (Hawaiian Language Immersion Program) was subsequently launched in 1987 with the approval of the Board of Education. Hawaiian language fluency and use has subsequently grown from threatened status to more than 8,000 second-language speakers and 1,000 native speakers (UCLA Language Materials Project). Hawaiians recently called for and were granted Board of Education approval for bilingual education in recognition of the indigenous language as a right and English as a literacy resource. While Hawaiians have gained political and educational ground over the last 40 years, Pacific Islander and Southeast Asian migrants to Hawai'i have not fared so well.

The state essentially experiences and maintains a historical legacy of private schools that favor speakers of "standard-like" English as opposed to Hawai'i Creole English and working-class immigrant native speakers of Pacific Islander and Filipino languages. While Hawaiians have legitimated their Hawaiian heritage through the elite private Kamehameha School and the public Ka Papahana Kaiapuni (Hawaiian immersion) schools, children from working-class immigrant homes tend to experience severely inadequate schooling (Davis, Cho, Ishida, Soria, & Bazzi, 2005). The high school graduation rate is slightly more than 50 percent for marginalized student populations (Green, 2002). Given these conditions, upper-, middle-, and even working-class parents tend to send their children to private schools for a better education. Immigrant children and youth clearly require quality bilingual/multilingual schooling for educational success through college. At the same time, these students potentially offer valuable future resources through providing for much needed interpretation and translation across professional and social services.

Engaging in Neoliberal Resistance

Davis draws on ELP in portraying the challenges that Hawai'i and other US states face in planning resistance to marginalizing policies and practices. The Hawai'i Council of Language Policy and Planning, developed in the early 1990s and composed of lawyers, educators, social service providers, community members, and nongovernmental organizations, was able to form a state government Language Access Office intended to facilitate much-needed interpretation and translation. Although the Council disbanded shortly thereafter due to an economic downturn that decimated funding needed to support nongovernmental organizations, efforts toward addressing inadequate language minoritized education were continued through federal grants.

Davis worked toward securing grants to support multilingual education for language minoritized student academic achievement through US DOE funding from 2001 to 2006 (Davis et al., 2005; Davis, 2009). In 2003, we drew on postmodern and multilingual theoretical principles in designing programs at a high school serving Filipino, Samoan, and Hawaiian students. Our federally funded *Studies of Heritage and Academic Languages and Literacies* (SHALL) elective program offered interactive courses in home/heritage languages, Pidgin/HCE, academic languages (English, Samoan, and Ilokano) and technology to more than 250 students. SHALL sought to promote linguistic and discursive proficiency, including improved understanding of school social and educational expectations. Students learned about and reflected on their hybrid heritage, local, and school identities and developed metalinguistic skills through language analyses. Academic English abilities were further fostered through year-long research projects that involved interviewing community members and teachers in Samoan, Ilokano, Hawai'i Creole English, and Standard English on issues of concern such as discrimination and standardized testing. They wrote critical research reports in academic English and produced public service announcements based on these reports that were broadcast on `Ōlelo Community Television. Compared to the national public school average of high school graduation rate of slightly more than 50 percent for marginalized student populations (Green, 2002), all SHALL student participants graduated from high school, and nearly 90 peercent went on to community colleges and universities. Yet this program was not continued by the high school nor promoted through the DOE.

A model of self-sustaining Hawaiian language immersion and Hawaiian and English bicultural/bilingual education was provided for in DOE Policy 2104 and 2105, respectively. These policies were the result of a state-wide Hawaiian sovereignty movement that allowed people who shared this common culture, religion, language, and value system to exercise control over their own lives. When the DOE initially resisted implementation of Hawaiian language immersion education, Hawaiians took to the streets in advocating for the right of educating their children in their heritage language. In winning this battle, the DOE's Hawaiian Kaiapuni programs are now offered at twenty schools that educate more than 2,000 students. Efforts to help ameliorate the current school crisis among immigrant students emerged through the Hawai'i Board of Education Policy 105.14 on Multilingual Education held on February 16, 2016 for "a full vote on adoption." Yet, after substantial revisions by the BOE, the goals subsequently stated in the policy are "to learn academic content and the official language medium of education, be it English or Hawaiian." There is no mention of bilingual education programs in Pacific Islander/other home languages in this policy. Subsequently, BOE 105.14 is likely to become a superficial approach in which teachers may allow home languages and discussion of cultural practices into the classroom but fail to realize bilingual instruction in children's home languages and English. For bilingual education to occur, Pacific Islanders most likely will need the support of Hawaiians and concerned others toward implementing all languages for instruction toward official bilingual education for all.

Discovering Alternatives: Countering Marginalizing Education

The Hawai'i Department of Education has historically created education policies and practices that discriminate against non-native speakers of Standard English, including speakers of both Hawai'i Creole English and marginalized home/community languages. Hawai'i public schools were charged in 1976, 1979, and 1999 for civil rights violations associated with neglecting the language and academic needs of immigrant students. These violations include the under-identification of language minorities, the lack of services for those who were identified, a disproportionate placement of language minorities in learning disabilities programs, inappropriate staffing of programs designed for language minoritized students, and improper mainstreaming procedures (Talmy, 2004). Pressing issues for the Hawai'i Department of Education are seemingly situated in the lack of knowledge and will to provide an informed language education program (Davis et al., 2005). US neoliberalism and national education policies have further conspired against providing schooling that is responsive to the language, identity, and agentive needs of diverse student populations. Lather (2004) argues that the "disciplining and normalizing effort to standardize educational research in the name of quality and effectiveness" (p. 26) shows, as Hall (1996) notes, an "aggressive resistance to difference (and) an assault, direct and indirect, on multiculturalism" (p. 468). An early study from the Harvard Civil Rights Project (Orfield, Losen, Wald, & Swanson, 2004) supported these observations in reporting nationwide student outcome data that indicate a "national crisis" in graduation rates of minoritized students. While *No Child Left Behind* policies have shifted to *Common Core Standards* that claim to promote inquiry skills across subject areas, this recent initiative may continue to create marginalizing education through states electing to use standardized curriculum and/or testing.

An opportunity for engaging in statewide policy and practices change emerged through the "Hawai'i Forum on Immigration and English Language Learners in Public Schools." This Forum, held in early 2014, was sponsored by the Hawai'i Educational Policy Center, the William S. Richardson School of Law, the College of Education, and School of Social Work at the University of Hawai'i, Mānoa. As an invited keynote speaker, Davis presented "Diversity in Crisis: Engaging Policies and Practices toward Educational Equity" which called for recognizing marginalized children's language/culture education rights and resources through a community-based Council on Language Policies and Plans. The Council subsequently promoted state-level administrator education and community-based advocacy by disseminating multilingual *Language Rights and Resources* information; organizing presentations to the BOE and DOE on multilingual education by well-known bilingual expert Ofelia García; and collectively discussing strategies for effective bilingual education in spring, 2015. Yet, as previously mentioned, the DOE superintendent, BOE, and University of Hawai'i College of Education have so far failed to establish an effective and comprehensive ESL/bilingual education program. One well-respected community elder and a respected educator observed that the current state of education for language minoritized students constitutes a form of institutionalized racism.

Community leaders in Hawai'i further reflect a local organizing movement through the recently formed coalition of Pacific Islanders who work toward recognition of their languages and cultures in public schools. This Hawai'i Community Language Council includes the creator and director of Le Fetuao Samoan Language Center, Elisapeta Alaimaleata, which provides approximately 300 parents, youth, and children with Samoan language preservation and development activities in Saturday schools. Other Community Language Council members include a representative of Micronesia who worked in education for 37 years as a classroom teacher and principal and is devoted to the education and home language preservation for all students; the vice president of the Chuuk Language and Cultural Association of Hawai'i who works toward the creation of schools on the islands of Micronesia and Chuuk and also served as a US congressman; an instructor of the Filipino language (Tagalog) at the University of Hawai'i, Mānoa who also speaks Ilocano and Cebuano. She further works with high school students toward "Early College Credit" at a local community college and directs a program for teaching the Filipino languages and culture to children at a Filipino Community Center; a Hawai'i Association of Language Teachers member who is dedicated to increased attention to linguistic diversity in the public schools; and University of Hawai'i graduate students who volunteer at Le Fetuao Samoan Language Center and participate in Council meetings. Davis also works with this group of advocates toward supporting bilingual/multilingual education in communities and public schools. While this community language project is in the early stages of development and planning, it holds potential for development and institutionalization of equitable language policies that meet the needs of all students.

Planning Effective Multilingual Policies and Practices

Current postmodern philosophy and theories promote deeper understanding of language and identity diversity, potentially leading to more effective and equitable policy and pedagogical practices that are locally situated and strategically employed (Cummins, 2006). García and Flores (2014) argue that while globalization has produced increased diversity as well as higher educational standards, contradictory forces of uniformity and diversity are creating educational tension, especially for educators of emergent bilingual students. Although the national Common Core State Standards at present do not allow for bilingual or multilingual education, García and Flores provide a highly convincing case for this inquiry and situated literacy form of schooling. They further promote translanguaging or the "soft assembling of multiple language practices in ways that fit a particular sociolinguistic situation" (García & Flores, 2014, p. 155) and argue for dynamic bilingualism and multifaceted identities that can be tremendous resources within the context of Common Core State Standards and for meeting global employment demands. Yet García and Flores (2014) also admit to the challenge of articulating an ongoing and individualized assessment of emergent bilingual students, given the vast diversity of their intersecting and ever-changing language, literacy, social/identities, and academic abilities. While emergent bilingual education and translanguaging (García & Li, 2014) is highly desirable in Hawai'i and elsewhere, students could be vulnerable to standardization as policy makers resist multilingual education. In addressing emergent multilingual schooling, we draw on the transnational work of teacher educators such as Portante and Max (2008) whose research on children's multilingualism and schooling in Luxembourg reveals that

> ...a range of tensions arise when the complex linguistic backgrounds of the children clash with normative, curriculum-oriented and teacher-centred instructional practices relying on textbooks and pre-structured activities. Nevertheless, these underlying tensions encourage teachers to transform their classroom practices to create innovative plurilingual classroom spaces that address the needs of changing population. Research data reveal that the children's linguistic and culturally diverse backgrounds work as resources for learning as they expand opportunities for participation and for learning of all children.
>
> (p. 124)

Hélot's (2007) "Ouverture aux Langues" approach in France also serves to enhance openness to "the other" and develop linguistic and cultural tolerance in schools toward language attitudes and practices that acknowledge global diversity. Vasco Correia's (2012) study focuses on language awareness implementation and outcomes in four primary school classrooms. Students were asked to tell stories about their language use, focusing on describing language networks, developing language landscapes, and creating language biographies. The goal is to help each student flourish in school via an emerging sense of community through heterogeneity. This ELP fieldwork provides rich and diverse data on an intervention that aims to sensitize students and teachers to multilingualism that exceeds and transforms official school language policies. Multilingual education advocates have worked to address both the challenges and possibilities of engaging in multilingual education. Yet policy makers worldwide often respond by arguing that a multilingual policy would not be feasible. For example, the Hawai'i Department of Education indicated that "(a multilingual) policy goes beyond the requirements of federal law by requiring the development and maintenance of students' home language." While there are no restrictions to going beyond federal law, their proposed position so far has denied the option of effective school-based bilingual/multilingual education.

Alternative Global/Local Programs and Schools

While focusing on language policy and planning, we suggest possibilities for school change through models of transformative education. As mentioned earlier, the 2011 book *A Match on Dry Grass: Community Organizing as a Catalyst for School Reform* by Mark Warren and Karen Mapp provides models of community school reform in San Jose, California; Los Angeles, California; Denver, Colorado; the Mississippi Delta; Chicago, Illinois; and West Bronx in New York City. A small-schools movement in Oakland, California provides a model for collaboration with school district officials as allies in developing more than forty schools that "…transformed the way education is provided in the district" (Warren & Mapp, 2011, p. 23). People Acting in Community Together in San Jose, California faced the challenges of 60 percent of students who were non-native speakers of English. School members built engagement through monthly community meetings that included parents, teachers, administrators, and students in decision making; 70 percent of the parents attended community meetings every month, and most were active in leadership roles such as interviewing teachers for employment at the school and serving as community liaisons. After two years of parent, student, and teacher involvement, the school was ranked the best performing in the district and the third-highest equivalent school in the state.

Another example of community-oriented schooling is the Citizen School in Porto Alegre, Brazil. Luis Gandin and Michael Apple (2002) describe forward-looking educators engaged in transformative schooling for those who live in poverty as well as others from working, middle, and professional classes. They provide ample evidence that democracy offers realistic alternatives to the "eviscerated version of thin democracy found under neoliberalism" (Porto Alegre City Secretariat of Education, 1999). They describe ways in which community schools can interrupt neoliberal and neoconservative policies and practices and build more fully democratic educational alternatives (Apple, 2001). The citizen school was "…created collectively, with active participation of teachers, school administrators and staff, students and parents in institutionalized forums of democratic decision making" (Gandin, 2006, p. 223). Thus, the Community School focused on democratization of management, access to the school, and access to knowledge.

> … (further) both the state agencies and the communities learn together to construct new mechanisms that represent the will of the communities…. Through thematic complexes, the students learn history by beginning with the historical experience of their families. They study important social and cultural content by focusing on and valorizing their own cultural manifestations….it is focused on real problems and interests of the students and the community.
> (Gandin & Apple, 2002, pp. 265, 267, 268)

The authors further hold that the inclusion of parents, students, support staff, and teachers in this process is one of the most innovative aspects of the model. In addition to contributing to collective curriculum development, municipal meetings of school councils provide a space where parents, students, teachers, and staff acquire the tools and construct the knowledge necessary to help administer the schools. Community schools thus give impoverished or otherwise marginalized populations a quality education that will enable them to have better chances in the paid labor market and at the same time operate as empowered citizens.

Conclusions

The rise of neoliberalism has prompted counter-social and educational equity movements that are geographically specific and globally relevant. We suggest here new directions in the language policy and planning/practices field toward engaged theories and methods that inform and transform (Tollefson, 2013). An engaged language policy approach moves toward articulating dialogic research approaches that acknowledge the harmful impact of global ideologies such as neoliberalism while building awareness of the potential for alternative local equitable policies and practices. This work seeks to model movement from a state of language and educational marginalization toward collective indigenous/minoritized and personal agency. Consciousness raising through ideological analysis and alternative equitable practices has further sought to help youth, villagers, and educators reevaluate and transform policies. Recognizing the agentive potential of ELP as an effective epistemological and methodological approach represents a substantive shift from seeing data as solely concrete and reportable to understanding data as also process and portrayable (Davis, 2014). In other words, although outcomes continue to be important to report, for the ELP researcher/learner, the process and the revealing of it take center stage. Drawing from Freire's dialogic process of conscientization, while making ideologies such as neoliberalism that underlie language policies and practices transparent and known, ELP also aims to raise consciousness among all the various actors involved in policy decision-making toward engagement in countering unjust practices. The cases of Nepal, Hawai'i, New York, California, Luxembourg, and Brazil represent on-the-ground work in differing states of addressing conscientization, resistance, and transformation. We further draw on critical ethnography as embedded in ELP to gain an understanding of participants' personal experience of history, place, and culture in relation to globalization, neoliberalism, and nationalism. We focus on how communities and indigenous/minoritized youth gain agency through dialectic processes intended to help construct, refine, and transform agency into action in resisting exclusionary language policies. We further intend to communicate a shift toward gaining knowledge about inequitable situations and providing models of exemplar equitable practices. Through portraying the processes of mutual engagement and/or resistance among relevant actors, we hope to further efforts toward realizing equity and human welfare. In these ways, ELP theoretical conceptualization and portrayal of engaged processes can help to foster collective commitment to and progress toward language and education social justice.

5
DEVELOPING RELEVANT AND ENGAGING LANGUAGE POLICIES AND PRACTICES

Scholars such as Blommaert and Rampton (2011), Creese and Blackledge (2010), and Lin (2013) reveal a profound shift in language policies and/or practices toward complexifying notions of language, identity, and the state. In recognizing post-structural and post-modern epistemological perspectives, they suggest that policy-making has moved from considering language education practices from the standpoint of homogeneity, stability, and boundedness toward concern with mobility, mixing, political dynamics, and historical embedding (Blommaert, 2014). These scholars further document ways in which nations manage language forms and practices as they align and disaffiliate with various groups as indication of their multiple and ever-changing identities and belongings. A growing sense of interactive local and global identities further rejects neoliberalism, embraces diversity, and resists inequitable policies and practices through taking up post-structuralist language and identity perspectives. This chapter first draws on transformative theories and practices toward addressing linguistic/educational inequality and then explores language policies/practices that support teachers in building on local knowledge for schooling that is relevant and engaging.

We then argue for investigating normative expectations in national education systems through the lens of post-structuralism and toward establishing the degree to which policy makers are committed to policing or receptive to change. Our ultimate goal is to promote locally based policies in which home languages and epistemologies of students are equally recognized and provided for in schooling. To these ends, this chapter explores the work of scholars (e.g., García, 2009; García & Flores, 2014; García & Li, 2014) who argue for emergent bilingual/multilingual education and call for translanguaging practices that promote educational equity. We further describe plurilingual educational practices in the United States, England, France, and South Africa that help students to flourish in school via an emerging sense of community and school language competence through heterogeneity. These practices seek to denaturalize dominant language ideologies that shape damaging or restrictive language policies and practices while working toward reimagining policies from multilingual perspectives. We further draw on García and Li (2014) and Hélot and O'Laoire (2011) in arguing for emergent bilingual/multilingual practices that support translanguaging toward socially just education. These and other scholars work toward helping each student flourish in school via an emerging sense of community and language competence through heterogeneity.

Translanguaging, Ideologies, and Multilingual Education

Recent critical studies reveal that multilingual language policies do not always promote students' actual language practices as reflected in local sociocultural/sociolinguistic contexts (Benson, 2013; Tupas, 2015). García (2009) specifically argues that transitional and additive models of bilingual education tend to reflect monolingual and monoglossic ideologies through compartmentalized language practices. For example, emergent bilinguals may struggle with language and content learning in spending half their time acquiring and using English while they learn in their home language the other half of the school day. More often, speakers of other than the authorized school languages are completely "submerged" in the official language(s). Such models fail to denaturalize monolingual nation-state and neoliberal ideologies that consider official and standard languages the norm for successful learning (Flores & García, 2013; Flores & Rosa, 2015). In calling for the denaturalization of compartmentalized language learning and use, scholars such as Benson (2013), Mohanty (2006), and Tupas (2015) explore equitable multilingual policy/practices that transform "monolingual habitus" that reproduces language hierarchies and unequal power relations (Benson, 2013). In other words, equitable multilingual education reimagines policies that embrace learners' dynamic language practices and multiple fluid identities across settings (García, 2009; Shohamy, 2006). Li and Zhu (2013) call for a "translanguaging ideology" that emerges from dialogic engagement with language policy actors toward reimagining multilingual education policies from learner and community perspectives. Lewis, Jones, and Baker (2012) further argue that translanguaging embraces a "…valued view of bilinguals (multilinguals) that relates to policy, planning, and politics at home and school, regionally and globally" (p. 625). These stances represent recent critical awareness of educational practices that acknowledge and build on multilingual learners' home language practices, cultural knowledge, and identities. An ideology of practice further develops through language policy actors' engagement with critical understanding of lived multilingual language experiences and ideological tensions embedded in historical, cultural, and political contexts (Li & Zhu, 2013).

Cen Williams (1994) initiated use of translanguaging as a pedagogical approach to teaching bilingual students. His method allowed students to receive input in one language (Welsh) and produce language in another language (English). García (2009) subsequently promoted translanguaging as "multiple discursive practices in which bilinguals engage in order to make sense of their bilingual [multilingual] worlds" (p. 45). She further advanced the position that translanguaging is intended to challenge nation-state and neoliberal ideologies that create language hierarchies; treat multilingualism as simply an additive process of learning two or more separate and autonomous languages; and diminish multilingual identities, voices, and agency through restrictive language policies and practices. Going beyond reproductionist policies and practices, translanguaging challenges sociolinguistic fractionalism and a diglossic view of language policy and planning (Lewis et al., 2012). However, multilingual experts suggest that translanguaging should not be understood simply as dynamic and fluid language practices that multilingual learners use to negotiate meanings and participate in social interaction. Li and Zhu (2013) and García and Li (2014) argue that a translanguaging ideology represents both critical and transformative language policies and practices. It is critical in that it challenges dominant monolingual ideologies. It is transformative because

> [i]t brings together different dimensions of the multilingual speakers' linguistic, cognitive, and social skills, their knowledge and experience of the social world and their attitudes and beliefs, and in doing so, develops and transforms the speakers' skills, knowledge, experience, attitudes, and beliefs; thus creating a new identity for the multilingual speaker.
> (Li & Zhu, 2013, p. 519)

In embracing multilingual learners' total linguistic repertoire as resources, translanguaging ideologies represent growing critical awareness of marginalizing ideologies and support the creation of inclusive and empowering language policies and practices. Thus, multilingual policies and practices promote a dynamic process through which students draw on existing linguistic and cultural knowledge, skills, ideologies, and agencies. In the following, we explore language policy initiatives that focus on promoting translanguaging policies and practices from the ground up.

Translanguaging in Complementary Schools

While mainstream education policies continue to impose unifying language ideologies as a response to increasing linguistic diversity (Blommaert, 2013), the rise of community-based complementary schools, particularly in the United Kingdom, has greatly contributed to promoting alternative or counter-public language ideologies, policies, and practices (e.g., Blackledge & Creese, 2010; Creese & Martin, 2008). In providing a safe space for minoritized languages, these schools recognize the role of teachers, community members, and students as transformative agents through personally experiencing and promoting equitable multilingual education policies and practices. Martin, Bhatt, Bhojani, and Creese (2006) further explore multilingual classroom practices of teachers and students in a Gujarati complementary school in the East Midlands city of Leicester, United Kingdom. Their study reveals that allowing students and teachers to use their multilingual practices in classrooms offers access to learning through drawing on their rich multilingual abilities. Such practices both challenge the dominant ideology that views multilingual practices as deficient pedagogical practice and creates a transformative space for multilingual learners to utilize existing linguistic and cultural resources. In another study, Creese, Bhatt, Bhojani, and Martin (2008) found that complementary schools recognize multilingual students' cultural and heritage language identities by privileging and encouraging them to reclaim these identities in the classroom. These studies show that flexible language policies and practices in complementary schools have been instrumental in engaging multilingual learners through exploring ethnic, linguistic, and cultural identities that allows them to recognize and draw on their multilingual learner identities, which include British varieties of English and multiple home languages (also see Archer, Francis, & Mau, 2009; Francis, Archer, & Mau, 2009). In these ways, language policies and practices are continuously engaged and co-constructed in the process of building on the rich linguistic and cultural knowledge of students, teachers, and supportive others. Through these models, monolingual and standard language ideologies are challenged and replaced by flexible multilingual language use.

Creese and Blackledge (2010) further adopt a collaborative ethnographic approach that engages teachers in creating space for children's multilingual practices in Bengali, Chinese, Gujarati, and Turkish complementary schools. This project contributes to raising teachers' awareness of and advocacy for translanguaging policies and practices that promote the linguistic and cultural identities of ethnic minoritized students. The project further highlights the need for going beyond an ideology of separate bi-/multilingualism and adopting a flexible multilingual approach toward addressing students' heritage, racial/ethnic, and linguistic identities and knowledge. Weber (2014) also argues that flexible multilingual education policies address multilingual children's needs and take their total linguistic repertoire as a resource for helping them to access school content. While challenging the essentialist and unitary ideologies of monolingual language policies, this approach further engages multilingual students and teachers in critical and inquiry-based understanding of sociocultural contexts that promote ideological awareness of what policies marginalize and what practices empower teachers and learners.

Creese and Blackledge (2010) also argue that complementary schools offer a flexible bilingualism that promotes language practices as heteroglossic in nature. Drawing on Bakhtin (1981), these researchers/supporters suggest that hybridity creates tension between unifying and diversifying ideologies, often resulting in positive multivoicedness. While embracing heteroglossia as a pedagogical approach, Blackledge and Creese (2014) claim that this method engages multilingual learners in gaining ideological awareness of sociopolitical, historical, ideological, and identity issues inherent in multilingual practices. Such awareness includes critical consciousness of power relations, multivoicedness, and linguistic plurality embedded in multilingual practices (Bailey, 2012; Kramsch, 2009). In the context of the complementary schools in the United Kingdom, Creese and Blackledge (2010) have identified the following major strategies that teachers have used to promote flexible multilingual policies and practices:

- Use of bilingual label quests, repetition and translation across languages.
- Ability to engage audiences through translanguaging and heteroglossia.
- Use of student translanguaging to establish identity positions both oppositional and encompassing of institutional values.
- Recognition that languages do not fit into clear bounded entities and that all languages are 'needed' for meanings to be conveyed and negotiated.
- Endorsement of simultaneous literacies and languages to keep the pedagogic task moving.
- Recognition that teachers and students skillfully use their languages for different functional goals such as narration and explanation.
- Use of translanguaging for annotating texts, providing greater access to the curriculum, and lesson accomplishment.

(pp. 112–113)

The flexible language policies and practices adopted in UK-based complementary schools build upon teachers' critical ideological awareness of what language policies address (or fail to address) in promoting multilingual students' agency and identities. As teachers engage in the planning and implementation process, they also participate in the process of ideological becoming that resists monolingualism. This process supports educators in creating space for translanguaging as a way in which multilingual students find safe spaces to negotiate their multiple worldviews, voices, and ideologies during the learning process (García, 2009; Hornberger & Link, 2012). In recognizing multilingual children's knowledge of history, heritage, culture, and community, teachers build on fluid multilingual practices as resources in education. Thus, translanguaging policies and practices in complementary schools uphold creativity, criticality, and transformation as key to equitable multilingual education policy (Blackledge & Creese, 2010; Li & Zhu, 2013). As Li (2011a) argues, creative multilingualism includes "pushing and breaking the boundaries between the old and the new, the conventional and the original, and the acceptable and the challenging" (p. 1223). In sum, criticality refers to "the ability to use available evidence appropriately, systematically and insightfully to inform considered views of cultural, social and linguistic phenomena, to question and problematize received wisdom, and to express views adequately through reasoned responses to situations" (Li, 2011a, p. 1223).

Li's (2011b) study of language practices in five complementary schools for British Chinese ethnic minoritized children in the United Kingdom clearly shows that equitable policies should address multilingual students' creative and critical use of their total linguistic repertoire in the learning process. His findings from Chinese complementary schools further support the idea of "multicompetence" (Cook, 1991), which challenges *One Language Only* or *One Language at a Time* ideologies. Language policies and practices in these complementary schools, as Li and Zhu (2013) witnessed, embrace multilingualism "as a window to human sociality, human cognition, social relations, and social structures" (p. 520). While engaging with translingual practices, these schools further allow students to use their language skills "to simultaneously follow and flout the rules and norms of behavior in the school" (Li, 2011b, p. 381). Yet such flexible language practices may challenge teachers' authority and their taken-for-granted ideology of teaching in a monolingual manner. Therefore, we argue for engaging multilingual teachers and students in dialogue concerning the tension among ideologies, policies, and histories (Kramsch, 2002) and, through this tension, develop creative and critical consciousness regarding language policies and practices.

Language policies in complementary schools are ultimately *engaged* in ideological becoming in three broad senses. First, these schools engage students, teachers, and parents in conversation toward promoting understanding of dominant language ideologies and their dehumanizing impact on social and educational experiences. Second, they provide ethnic students with opportunities to use their existing linguistic and cultural skills in both formal and informal venues. Thus, they provide communities, teachers, and students a safe dialogic space, which Li (2011a) calls a "translanguaging space," where multilingual students not only invest in their "capacity to use multiple linguistic resources to form and transform their own lives" but also create a "third space" (Bhabha, 1994) through which they experience transformative power (see Li, 2011a, p. 1223). Third, within this dialogic space, multiple ideologies, identities, values, and language practices do not simply coexist, but new ideologies, identities and practices are created through engagement in translingual spaces in schools. Moreover, these complementary schools are transformative in nature; they recognize agency, activism, and ideologies of ethnic minoritized students, teachers, and communities. In the words of Li and Zhu (2013), language policies and practices in these schools are transformative because the act of translanguaging

> ...brings together different dimensions of the multilingual speakers' linguistic, cognitive, and social skills, their knowledge and experience of the social world and their attitudes and beliefs, and in doing so, develops and transforms the speakers' skills, knowledge, experience, attitudes, and beliefs; thus creating a new identity for the multilingual speaker.
> (p. 519)

In sum, translanguaging policies and practices in these complementary schools not only ensure the use of multilingual learners' existing linguistic and cultural knowledge and skills but recognize their multilingual identities, ideologies, and voices as legitimate means to access both local and global resources (Blackledge & Creese, 2010; Hornberger & Link, 2012). In engaging in deeper understanding of teaching content through co-construction of meaning and collaborative inquiry, these schools recognize multilingual learners as experts and agents for their own learning. Li (2014) has shown that translanguaging policies break down power relations and create a collaborative learning environment that encourages teachers and students to learn from one another. While engaging in this process, multilingual learners further create new ideologies and consciousness that resist linguistic hierarchies and inequalities while building agency and activism toward ensuring multilingual practices in schools.

Translanguaging for Social Justice

Recent studies have focused on how translanguaging practices may contribute to policy transformation toward socially just education. Going beyond the conceptualization of translanguaging as a pedagogical strategy, García and Leiva (2014) specifically point out that "our understanding of dynamic bilingualism and flexible language use must impact education policies that continue to insist on monolingual standards to educate and especially to assess" (p. 214). To this end, these scholars argue that students must be "engaged in translanguaging discourses and teachers must value translanguaging and build on those flexible practices" to educate all children (Garcia & Leiva, 2014, p. 214). As translanguaging discourses expose students to alternative histories, representations, and knowledge, translanguaging policies have the "potential to burst the 'standard language' bubble in education that continues to ostracize many bilingual students, and most especially immigrants" (García & Leiva, 2014, p. 125). Thus, García and Li (2014) view translanguaging as transformative social action that not only helps students to understand the content of teaching but calls "forth bilingual [multilingual] subjectivities and sustaining bilingual [multilingual] performances that go beyond one or the other binary logic of two autonomous languages" (pp. 92–93). Translanguaging is transformative in that it recognizes students' linguistic strengths and "reduces the risk of alienation at school by incorporating languaging and cultural references familiar to language-minoritized students" (García & Li, 2014). Most important, translanguaging "*transgresses and destabilizes* language hierarchies, and at the same time *expands and extends* practices that are typically valued in school and in the everyday world of communities and homes" (García & Li, 2014, p. 68). In other words, translanguaging does not simply include simultaneous use of multiple languages but is an act of transforming inequitable linguistic histories, essential linguistic boundaries, and an ideology of contempt toward minoritized languages. Language policies that embrace this libratory perspective build on multilingual students' and teachers' agencies, knowledge, and critical understanding of local/global socio-historical conditions.

García and Sylvan (2011) further discuss efforts to engage US newcomer immigrants in activities that promote agency and home language expertise while providing opportunities for meaning-making processes toward learning English for both academic and social purposes. Through this process, multilingual students learn from both English-speaking peers and multimedia resources such as iPads and Google Translate. As facilitators, teachers in bilingual programs are also language learners rather than solely linguistic authorities. Through teacher/student translingual practices, multilingual students are able to generate multiple perspectives on topics of discussion and negotiate skills and identities toward performing classroom tasks. García and Sylvan (2011) argue that these programs are successful in promoting plurilingual pedagogy that raises student awareness of language heterogeneity, student-teacher collaboration, learner-centeredness, language-content integration, inclusivity of languages, experiential learning, and local autonomy.

Hornberger and Link (2012) further discuss implications of translanguaging practices for language policy transformation. Building on biliteracy and multiliteracy perspectives, they argue that translanguaging provides important insights into reformulating language education policy and practices toward promoting better and more equitable education experiences. While discussing the negative impact of an English-only ideology and standardized testing, they maintain that it is important to raise awareness among students, teachers, and policy makers that translanguaging and transnational literacies are necessary for empowering *all* children. Hornberger and Link (2012) argue that "fluid, multilingual, oral, contextualized practices and voices in educational policy and practice becomes an even more powerful imperative for contesting the social inequalities of language" (Hornberger & Link, 2012, p. 265). Their study shows that engaging multilingual learners in translanguaging practices valorizes and validates home language literacies, funds of knowledge, identities, and ideologies as resources.

García and Leiva (2014) describe the ways in which an English language arts teacher, Camila, draws on her own bilingual resources to promote effective translanguaging with emergent bilingual Spanish-speaking students. She further illustrates the ways in which this multilingual classroom policy and connected practices engage teachers and students in enacting social transformation. This process not only aims to eliminate linguistic hierarchies but, most importantly, releases them (US Latinos) from the constraints of either Spanish/English monolingualism or a static additive bilingualism (p. 205). The school Camila teaches at is a government-funded high school designed for immigrant newcomers to New York City. Going beyond the traditional notion of second language and English as a second language programs, this school allows immigrant students to use their home language practices in making sense of the learning processes they are immersed in. The students of this school are mostly from Ecuador and come from working-class families. Students have differential Spanish and English language proficiency and have resided in the United States from 6 months to more than a year.

Camila's translanguaging takes a multilingual and multiliteracy approach (Street, 1995, 2000) designed to build on minoritized and vernacular ways of speaking, reading, and writing that include poems, plays, and stories written at home and in other everyday non-school contexts (Hornberger & Link, 2012, p. 268). Thus, rather than privileging monolingual and standard language literacies, translanguaging engages multilingual learners in multicultural, multilingual and multimodal literacy skills to promote equitable multilingualism. García and Leiva (2014) describe Camila's use of translanguaging as a "mechanism for social justice, especially when teaching students from language minoritized communities" (p. 200). This teacher's translanguaging approach further includes student activities such as watching and listening to bilingual (Spanish-English) hip-hop music videos and translating the lyrics. The music videos reveal everyday struggles of Latino immigrants that include police brutality, fear of deportation and arrest, and a sense of being excluded and marginalized. For example, one rap music video shows police identifying and arresting an "illegal" immigrant Latino man who had been watching his wife lovingly feed their son. As the child and mother begin to cry, the scene shifts to a white middle-class family enjoying a peaceful meal. Yet the video further illustrates the collective resistance of Latino immigrants through displaying an image of children and their parents displaying posters with counter-messages in both English and Spanish of resistance to anti-illegal immigration. The counter-message reads, "4 million US citizen children are fighting to keep their Moms and Dads" (García & Leiva, 2014, p. 208). The video ends with "Unidos todos con esta cancion. Si se pued" (United with this song, yes we can).

Dialogue is a central part of Camila's translanguaging pedagogy. After watching bilingual videos, students engage in dialogue that critically explores the issues they viewed. Students use both English and Spanish to participate in conversation through which they develop critical awareness concerning the history of linguistic, political, and cultural oppression in the United States. García and Leiva (2014) suggest that Camila's dialogic engagement not only legitimates students' dynamic language practices but, most important, produces a new subjectivity among Latino children. This subjectivity includes alternative knowledge and consciousness that represents immigrant students' histories, knowledge, and discourses (also García & Li, 2014). Through engaging in analyzing tension between an English-only ideology and bilingual practices evident in videos, the students developed a new ideology that constitutes liberating action from historical and linguistic oppression. In confronting inequitable ideologies and discourses about language, politics, and privilege, these students were further able to reclaim alternative knowledge and voices that had been silenced by an ideology of monolingual American nationalism (Flores & García, 2013; Wiley, 2004).

García and Leiva's (2014) study clearly shows that dialogic engagement contributes to the ideological becoming (Bakhtin, 1981) of multilingual learners. Through translingual dialogic engagement, the students come into "contact with others that is always unfinished and unfinishable, thus, enabling the possibilities of acting for social justice" (p. 202). In this sense, translanguaging is not just about the mixing of hybrid cultures and languages; rather, it is a "new way of being, acting and languaging" that gives "voice to new social realities" (p. 204). In other words, translanguaging constitutes social practices and actions that seek to transform the status quo of linguistic hierarchies. This is indeed a product of border and subaltern resistance to the asymmetries of power that "bilingual codes often create" (García & Leiva, 2014, p. 204). García and Leiva (2014) have found that engaging in translanguaging practices serves to unravel subjugated histories and move minoritized students toward ideological becoming. As minoritized students become aware of ideological tensions, they often further engage in activist and advocacy work for social justice.

In a study of dialogic engagement, Flores and García (2013) discuss how two teachers at the Pan American International High School in New York use translanguaging strategies to create a linguistic "third space" (Bhabha, 1994) for multilingual Latino students. These teachers use translanguaging as a way to engage students in dialogue toward deeper understanding of sociopolitical conditions of oppression. This third space further allows students to denaturalize colonial ideologies of language as a homogeneous, fixed, and unitary system. Translanguaging not only helps multilingual students make sense of what they are learning but engages them in critical analysis of sociopolitical issues, histories and counter-histories, social injustice, and linguistic and cultural oppression. In this sense, teachers' translanguaging with students supports both effective learning and social justice. By using their own dynamic language and cultural practices, multilingual learners challenge both monolingual education and compartmentalization of languages in bilingual education. In other words, translanguaging practices deconstruct hierarchies of languages in education policies and practices, including multilingual education, to ensure "full participation of all citizens, including those who are linguistically different" (Flores & García, 2013, p. 255).

Makalela (2014) also engages student teachers in promoting multilingual development at the University of the Witwatersrand, South Africa. In critiquing a history of compartmentalization of languages, Makalela adopts translanguaging policies toward educating student teachers in the use of languages that successfully serve their future students. More specifically, these student teachers learn Sepedi as an additional language so as to be fully prepared to teach students who are speakers of this language. For example, one course for student teachers focused on development of basic Sepedi conversation, reading, and writing through which participants engaged in using technology and social media such as Facebook and blogs. While student teachers learned to read and write Sepedi, they were free to express ideas in any languages they felt comfortable speaking. They further engaged in writing reflective multilingual blogs in Sepedi, their home language, and English. These student teachers subsequently not only began to understand the relevance of translanguaging in learning a new language, but they increasingly developed multicultural awareness. For example, they became aware of the Sepedi language used in death, wedding, and burial procedures and, through this process, began to develop awareness of fluid cultural and linguistic boundaries that are important for culturally appropriate multilingual education.

A translanguaging approach not only helped student teachers develop Sepedi language competence but provided the means to acquire critical awareness of the commonalities and interconnectedness among languages such as Sepedi, Sesotho, and Setswana. This particular translanguaging approach further represented an African worldview of *Ubuntu,* which is based on the principle of community orientation and interconnectedness. While engaging in translanguaging practices, these student teachers dismantled past ethnolinguistic hierarchies of language and subsequently promoted a pedagogy of integration (García, 2012). While debunking a monolingual approach to teaching African languages, these student teachers engaged in a process of liberating historically excluded languages and affirm fluid identities. In another study, Ramani and Joseph (2010) explored how students engaged in a bilingual B.A. program at the University of Limpopo in South Africa through translanguaging and transnational literacies. In this program, students used translanguaging for developing both spoken and written skills in Sepedi and other local varieties of South African English to engage in classroom discussion. Most important, these students explored both the private speech of Sepedi-speaking children and language practices throughout the community. Through this experience, student teachers become aware of the value of their own home language/culture and, thus, begin to understand the importance of affirming other multilingual and multicultural identities.

In sum, translanguaging is not just about language pedagogy but also, and most important, about language policy transformation from the bottom up. It provides multilingual learners, teachers, and parents space for dialogue in which they unravel concealed histories of oppression and develop ideological awareness toward social activism and advocacy for equitable and meaningful education (García & Li, 2014). Translanguaging further represents locally situated practice-based language policy that "opens up a space of resistance and social justice" by breaking down the racialized and stigmatized beliefs about multilingual practices of minoritized and indigenous people (García & Li, 2014, p. 115). In other words, translanguaging represents multilingual learners' ideological awareness and social action that resists monolingual ideologies and language hierarchies (Blommaert, 2010; Makoni & Pennycook, 2005) and re-imagines equitable multilingual education (García, 2009; Li, 2014). Translanguaging validates multilingual learners' language practices as legitimate and rejects an ideology of linguistic contempt (Dorian, 1994, 1998; Farr & Song, 2011) toward valuing minoritized languages and language practices. While recognizing the importance of minoritized languages in school and society, translanguaging engages multilingual learners in becoming aware of ideological complexities that result from their contact with people with different linguistic and cultural backgrounds that further "releases histories and understandings that had been buried within fixed language identities constrained by nation-states" (García & Li, 2014, p. 21). This means that, as Li (2011a) and Velasco and García (2014) argue, translanguaging breaks down artificial linguistic and cultural borderlands and creates a dialogic space in which multilingual learners bring "their personal history, experience and environment, their attitudes, beliefs and ideologies, their cognitive and physical capacity into one coordinated and meaningful performance" (Li, 2011a, p. 1223). In sum, engaging students in and through translanguaging supports minoritized language speakers' ideological becoming toward legitimizing their identities, knowledge, and historical conditions as resources rather than problems toward equitable multilingual education.

Identity Investment, Multicompetence and Multilingual Policy

In this section, we explore grassroots practices and activism that engage multilingual learners and teachers toward challenging an essentialist nation-state identity and embracing hybrid linguistic and cultural identities that support equitable education. Identity has been a major topic of discussion in language policy (Blommaert, 2006; Heller, 2010; Tsui & Tollefson, 2007) and language education (Block, 2007; Norton, 2000). In considering identity, both imagined and real, as key to shaping language policies and practices, we view identities not as monolithic but as fluid, context-sensitive, and discursively constructed social processes (Anzaldúa, 1987; Bhabha, 1994; Pavlenko & Blackledge, 2004). These and other studies have also critiqued the negative impact of essentialist nation-state identity on multilingual children's educational experiences (Blommaert, 2006; Shohamy, 2006). Going beyond nation-state identity, there is increased interest in embracing the multiplicity and fluidity of identity in language policy and practices toward recognizing minoritized language use in education and other public spheres. As Holt and Gubbins (2002, p. 4) argue, such a perspective helps "to link or acknowledge the past in light of a different cultural environment rather than a mark of disloyalty" (as cited in García, 2009). Furthermore, scholars (e.g., García & Sylvan, 2011; Hornberger & McCarty, 2012) argue that language policies should focus on multilingual learners' historical, political, linguistic, and socioeconomic identities and engage them in the process of understanding why the multilingual identities they construct are important resources for inclusive and equitable multilingual education.

The work of Cummins (2005, 2006) and Cummins and Early (2010) on multilingual learners' "identity texts" and "identity investment" provides important insights into engaging policy makers, teachers, and parents in creating transformative space for linguistic diversity in the face of increased English language dominance in education worldwide. Building on his collaborative work with educators in the Greater Toronto Area of Canada, Cummins (2006) argues that policy makers and educators must first and foremost create pedagogical and interpersonal space for multilingual learners' *identity investment* that greatly affects cognitive engagement in learning processes. Identity investment is based on the view that students can effectively learn when they are provided with opportunities to negotiate their identities, understand societal power relations, and invest in acquiring linguistic, cultural, and social capital through a multilingual learning process (see also Block, 2006; Norton, 2000). To this end, Cummins (2006) collaborated with educators toward engaging multilingual learners in developing "identity texts" that are "the products of students' creative work or performances carried out within [a] pedagogical space" (p. 60). While students invest in various speaking identities, teachers "then hold a mirror up to students in which their identities are reflected back in a positive light" (Cummins, 2006, p. 60). In other words, student performances of multilingual spoken, written, visual, musical, and dramatic texts provide these learners with the artistic means by which they feel valued rather than deficient as multilingual learners. More specifically, in working on identity texts, students use their home language literacy skills, build on their personal lived experiences and sociopolitical realities, and use multimodal technologies to reach wider audiences. For example, three Pakistani multilingual immigrant children, with different levels of English and Urdu language proficiency, collaborated on a story-writing project. For several weeks, these children worked together, with teacher support, to write a story about *The*

New Country that recounts their own experiences of migration from Pakistan to Canada. Although the students dominantly used Urdu to discuss topics and characters, they drew on English to write initial drafts of their stories. Through this process, these children learned Urdu and English from each other toward fully participating in the production of their identity texts. The students also became increasingly aware of power relations between languages and were subsequently proud of being able to author a bilingual story book that represents their multiple linguistic, personal, and social identities (Cummins & Early, 2010).

Theories and practices concerning identity investment further provide significant insight into reimagining an equitable multilingual education policy. First, as argued by Cummins (2006) and Cummins and Early (2010), the legitimization of children's home languages and social capital is the most essential part of multilingual education. As revealed in the identity texts project, an equitable multilingual policy requires breaking down linguistic boundaries toward embracing multiliteracy that creates space for learners' identity investment (Baker, 2011; Street, 1995). Thus, students begin to see the importance of their own home language in learning English for academic purposes and, thus, liberates them from a dominant language ideology that commonly views minoritized languages as "inappropriate" in education (Blommaert, 2005; Irvine & Gal, 2000; Silverstein, 2000). Thus, multilingual learners' engagement in identity texts proves to be an empowering and transformative means for promoting multilingualism from the ground up.

Cummins' (2005) identity investment further supports the notion of "multicompetence" (Cook, 1991) or an individual's knowledge of more than one language and corresponding socio-academic abilities. As a holistic concept to describe multilingual learners' language ability, multicompetence embraces dynamic use of translanguaging as part of the usual linguistic repertoire of multilingual learners. In other words, recognition of learners' home languages and varied linguistic abilities is likely to ensure their effective participation in learning. Cummins' studies further show that it is important to educate the educators to promote linguistic and cultural sensitivity toward all the languages and language practices that students bring to the classroom. For example, schools should recognize children's home and community language practices as resources, and encourage them to negotiate and perform multiple identities. As Hélot and Young (2006) argue, a multilingual school is a place

> [...]where linguistic and cultural diversity is acknowledged and valued, where children can feel safe to use their home language alongside the school language ...to learn and to communicate, where teachers are not afraid and do not feel threatened to hear languages they do not know, and where multilingualism and multilingual literacies are supported.
>
> (p. 69)

Thus, a multilingual school cannot be imagined without breaking down discriminatory "borders" of language, culture, and identity. In sum, Cummins's conceptualization of identity investment serves to engage educators and students in resisting monolingual ideologies and create safe spaces for negotiating and investing in multiple identities. In the following, we further discuss engaged studies that focus on alternative ideologies and language policy transformation.

Critical Language Awareness and Pedagogy of the Possible

While acknowledging the ideological complexities inherent in multilingualism and multilingual language policy, recent studies have emphasized the importance of engagement with teachers, parents, and students toward denaturalizing traditional monolingual habitus from the bottom up (e.g., García & Menken, 2010; Hélot & Young, 2006; Hélot & O'Laoire, 2011). As Hélot and O'Laoire argue, efforts toward reimagining multilingualism in school

> …must take into account the complex ecologies at stake, as well as the complex interrelationships between local and global agendas and the extent to which local actors are aware of their own agency, or prepared to become agents of change engaged in contesting the power relationships in place.
>
> (p. xvii)

Engaging teachers, parents, students, and other concerned language policy actors in contesting hegemonic ideologies contributes to a new pedagogy: a pedagogy of the possible. For Hélot and O'Laoire (2011), a *pedagogy of the possible* means that

> [R]ather than responding to the exigencies of the multilingual classroom in a *negative way* and waiting for centralist policies to decree new objectives, the notions of ecology and *agency* invite teachers and learners to see their realities in a new light and to act on this reality: in other words, to respond to all possibilities and potentialities at the classroom level, thus forging one's own policies that are locally effective and empowering.
>
> (p. xvii, emphasis added)

A pedagogy of the possible builds on critical awareness of teachers, students, parents, and others concerned about sociopolitical inequalities, marginalizing ideologies, and their own agency and activism toward transforming hegemonic ideologies and practices. Similar to Freire's (1992) *pedagogy of hope,* which supports progressive post-modernity, liberation, tolerance, inclusion, and empowerment, a pedagogy of the possible seeks to develop agency and activism by engaging teachers, students, and parents in critical dialogue through various collaborative actions (Giroux, 1997; hooks, 2003). A pedagogy of the possible further rejects the nation-state ideology and embraces local multilingualism and cultures as resources for education.

Engaging language policy actors in creating a pedagogy of the possible for multilingualism lies in developing *critical language awareness* among all concerned. This approach goes beyond traditional language consciousness (Hawkins, 1984) toward seeking to engage multiple actors—teachers, parents, students, administrators—in understanding power relations and critiquing sociopolitical inequalities embedded in language use and practices (Clark & Ivanic, 1992; Fairclough, 1992; Farías, 2005). Achugar (2015, p. 1) further argues that engagement in "explicit discussion of power issues in the contexts of literacy and language instruction" deals with the political nature of language policy and aims to build agency and activism toward social transformation. Corson (1999) maintains that teachers, administrators, parents, and experts must gain critical awareness of schooling injustices and collaborate in developing policies that address linguistic and sociocultural marginalization reflected in schooling practices. In supporting minoritized language schooling, Corson (1999) contends that students should engage in critical dialogue concerning racism, bias, prejudice, and linguistic discrimination in schools and beyond. This engagement can lead to student critical awareness of complex linguistic/cultural diversity as enriching rather than problematic.

Critical language awareness approaches most often engage language policy actors in resisting and transforming hegemonic ideology from the bottom up. For example, despite monolingual habitus rooted in French nationalism, Hélot and Young (2006) and Young and Hélot (2008) adopt a language awareness approach that reimagines an inclusive and plurilingual policy in French schools. Their Didenheim School Project aims to address ideological challenges created by a French monolingual ideology toward promoting linguistic and cultural diversity as school resources. Through collaboration with ideologically aware parents, teachers, and students, schools promote pedagogic activities that further raise positive multilingual awareness among students and all concerned (García, 2008; Hawkins, 1984). For example, Hélot and Young draw on parents as key agents for creating multilingual space through visiting schools as experts of multiple languages and cultures. Students are encouraged to ask a wide range of questions, and parents engage students in a variety of activities such as learning home language songs; experiencing a variety of foods; learning cultural politeness rules; understanding the geography and history of migration; and reading, writing, and comparing different languages. Through this process, children became aware of the need to recognize and embrace linguistic diversity in schools and beyond. Commenting on what her child learned from this project, a Turkish mother states,

Before, my children had problems with other children, but since I have given the class about Turkish, every time we meet children from the class, they say to me, they want to speak to me, but before it was different, now they even say the word, they say "merhaba", some of them say hello, I'm happy.

(Hélot & Young, 2006, p. 82)

Both parents and teachers also saw the value of diversity as "collective resources for all" (Hélot & Young, 2006, p. 83). For example, a year-2 teacher "sees her class as a small community of learners who need to understand what it means to live and work together" (Hélot & Young, 2006, p. 83). In another study, Hélot (2011) engaged French primary teachers in analyzing translated bilingual and dual-language children's literature toward recognizing multi-literacies. As a whole, this diversity project highlights the significance of engaging parents, teachers, and students in collaborative action and dialogue toward raising multilingual awareness in schools (Hélot, 2011). In sum, it promotes linguistic diversity and plurilingual practices that move beyond *monoglossic ideologies* and *two solitudes models* of bilingual education (Cummins, 2007; García, 2009). As the teachers critically analyzed representations of languages in translated textbooks, they became aware of how languages represent a particular culture and community and began to see the need to recognize interdependence between languages in diverse environments (Baker, 2011). Most important, teachers have the ability to see value in translanguaging and translation as ways in which multiliteracy skills and plurilingual education are promoted in the classroom.

In building on a critical language awareness approach (Fairclough, 1999; Hawkins, 1984), García (2008) conceptualizes *multilingual language awareness* (MLA) as a way to engage teachers, students, and schools in understanding social, political, and economic manifestations of multilingual language practices. She defines MLA as "the understanding of the social, political and economic struggles surrounding the use of the two [or more] languages" (pp. 387–388). MLA focuses on awareness of how languages are used in "undemocratic ways to exclude and discriminate" (Shohamy, 2006, p. 182). García (2008) has engaged teachers in various ways to raise their awareness of multilingual differences and reimagine pedagogy that deconstructs monolingual and standard language ideologies. She describes six different strategies for engaging teachers in MLA. In the *Descriptive Review of a Bilingual Child's Language Use*, she suggests that teachers engage in exploring and describing complexities surrounding children's multilingual language practices in different domains. Teachers are also engaged in documenting languages in public signs, newspapers, and magazines by using photographs and videos. They also interview community leaders and parents about their sociopolitical and economic struggles and gather data about institutions supporting minoritized languages and the struggles they face in doing so. Moreover, teachers also collect funds of knowledge from the community and teachers. While analyzing the authentic data they gathered, these teachers become aware of sociopolitical issues concerning multilingual differences. They also use these data to provide explicit instruction to students about multilingual practices in society.

García (2008) further engages teachers in close observation and description of how language and literacy is used by the teacher and the students in the classroom. The teachers then analyze how particular language practices and discourses are used in different contexts and purposes such as class arrangements, lessons, assignments, and testing. While collaboratively analyzing language and literacy practices in the classroom, the teachers also compare language practices they have collected from outside classroom. This encourages teachers to transform what is not working for their multilingual classroom and to embrace what is helpful for their students. The teachers then produce multilingual and multilingual texts that include their own personal experiences of linguistic and cultural understandings and then share these texts with their colleagues. They then engage in dialogue that generates multiple understandings about the texts they produce. As these teachers become aware of children's language practices, sociopolitical aspects of the speech community, and complexities of the multilingual classroom, they further engage in developing multicultural and multilingual curricula for their classes. They also try out curricula and engage in reflection and transformation of practices. Having a greater "ideological clarification" about language issues, the student teachers often become social activists. They transform their ideological awareness into action; they help families with translation services and sometimes participate in advocating for transforming national policies. They further organized a letter campaign, participated in radio programs, and spoke to politicians about the inequities and struggles of immigrants learning English.

Yet, critical language awareness is not just about multilingual awareness. It is also concerned with supporting ongoing grassroots activism and advocacy toward ensuring multilingual education that represents school demographics. Leeman, Rabin, and Román-Mendoza (2011) adopt a critical language awareness approach to engaging college Spanish heritage language (SHL) speakers in activism that counters school-based subordination of SHL in the United States. While focusing on identity, agency, and advocacy as key components of language activism, they contend that monolingual ideology and institutionalization of linguistic subordination "not only can lead to lowered self-esteem and a sense of disempowerment, but it also reinforces linguistic discrimination and reduces the chances of attaining education and societal success" (Leeman et al., 2011, p. 482). Their action research involves college students in a *critical service-learning program* designed to teach SHL and literacy skills to young learners in a public elementary school. Dialogue is the major component of the program. Student teachers engaged in dialogic processes with community members toward collectively exploring and discussing ideological issues surrounding SHL. In the after-school reading and writing classes, student teachers invited Spanish-speaking parents as guest lecturers and discussants toward acknowledging sociopolitical issues concerning SHL. They also developed online tools such as wiki and blog to critically reflect on what they learned in engagement with teaching SHL and engaging in dialogue with parents and youth.

Leeman et al. (2011) argue that engaging pre-service education students in critical service learning raises their awareness of language ideologies and policies created through promotion of one-language-one-nation stances. Students thus not only gain expertise in promoting heritage language and literacy skills but become aware of the need to embrace their own identities as expert, activist, and advocate for home and heritage language education. While further embracing their identity as activists, the student teachers challenged the dominant language ideology present in schools and communities that consider SHL speakers "limited" or "deficient" learners. In sum, student teachers have the ability and the right to engage in critical activism and ideological awareness by participating in dialogue with communities and utilizing their knowledge and skills in school settings toward promoting equitable and socially just language education policy.

Through collaborative action research, Huberman (2001) and Wallen and Kelly-Holmes (2015) engaged Republic of Ireland teachers in dialogue toward promoting awareness of the need for bilingual education in children's Irish home language and English as an additional language. In countering an English-only policy, these advocates used dialogue as a method of critical consciousness-raising that built on teachers' own language experiences along with theories of bilingual education and second language learning. Wallen and Kelly-Holmes' (2015) study revealed that collaborative dialogue in which teachers are given opportunities to discuss both dominant and alternative ideologies of language learning promoted teachers' critical reflection on their own practices and assumptions toward developing alternative perspectives on bilingualism. For example, Tara, one of the participants, began to see the value of students' home language through learning that "…if the pupil has already succeeded in their first language, it will mean faster progress with a second language" (Wallen & Kelly-Holmes, 2015, p. 9). This dialogic inquiry process implies that engaging teachers in explicit and critical analysis of ideologies and experiences contributes to transforming an ideology of contempt toward the use of students' home languages in school toward promoting multilingual and multiliteracy education in the classroom.

Community Engagement and Funds of Knowledge

Community engagement and funds of knowledge (González, Moll, & Amanti, 2005; Moll, Amanti, Neff, & González, 1992) have received ongoing attention in language education programs for *all* language minoritized children (Benson,

2005; García & Kleifgen, 2010; Skutnabb-Kangas & Heugh, 2012). Moll et al. (1992) defined funds of knowledge as "the historically accumulated and culturally developed bodies of knowledge and skills essential for household or individual functioning and well-being" (p. 133). Such knowledge is rooted in local sociocultural practices and considered key resources for community development. Although such knowledge is often erased from mainstream curricula, textbooks, and pedagogical practices (García & Kleifgen, 2010), recent creation of mother tongue-based multilingual education policies address increased dropout and educational underachievement through recognizing the importance of local funds of knowledge (see Kosonen & Young, 2009; Skutnabb-Kangas, Phillipson, Mohanty, & Panda, 2009).

In efforts to further support multilingual education policies from the bottom up, advocates have recently conceptualized the notion of *critical indigenous pedagogy* (Hough, Thapa-Magar, & Yonjan-Tamang, 2009). Building on Freirian theory and Moll et al.'s *Funds of Knowledge*, critical indigenous pedagogy reflects local ways of knowing, being, and doing. This pedagogy utilizes *indigenous critical praxis* that promotes indigenous reflection on their culture, history, knowledge, and sociopolitical condition (Gegeo & Watson-Gegeo, 2002, 2013) toward a critical indigenous pedagogy that empowers indigenous people and embraces their role as sources of knowledge and agency. Thus, this pedagogy not only ensures participation of the community in educational activities but validates indigenous ways of learning, being, and knowing. Hough et al. (2009) engaged Tamang community members, who represent one of the most sociopolitically marginalized indigenous communities in Nepal, in creating and promoting multilingual education in public schools. With an aim to promote the use of Tamang in school, these language activists utilized a critical indigenous approach that drew on traditional values, epistemologies, and critical awareness of the world in dialectic relationship. Toward empowering Tamang teachers and community members, Hough et al. (2009) organized workshops for teachers from two public schools in the rural Rasuwa district. Participants first engaged in developing generic themes for developing culturally appropriate learning and teaching materials. These themes included herbal medicines and learning practices; traditional and modern knowledge and skills; history, numerical, and measurement systems; religious practices and belief systems; and rituals, festivals, songs, and poems. Teachers and community members then were involved in documenting various plants, roots, vines, and so on; health care and healing practices; songs; and stories. Throughout this process, participants engaged in critical dialogue about why rich indigenous knowledge is not given space in education and, thus, maintained for future generations. The participants further engaged in critically contrasting the traditional and modern knowledge system within communities. Indigenous parents revealed that local crops and agriculture practices are threatened by recent introduction of pesticides and importation of often unhealthy processed foods. Teachers and community members further increasingly understand the importance of locally grown plants used to produce pots, bags, and containers that are gradually being replaced by plastic bags.

In considering community as a source of knowledge and a key agent for language policy creation, implementation, and transformation, Laviña-Gumba (2015) describes community engagement in indigenous language and literacy programs in Western Subanon and Binukid/Higaonon communities of the Philippines. Building on both funds of knowledge and Freire's (1970) dialogue and praxis perspectives, literacy programs have aimed at empowerment through drawing on community funds of knowledge in the areas of health, nutrition, small-scale industries, local culture, and ancestral practices as major components of the school curriculum. Community members further engage in research, advocacy, training, orthography development and materials creation, class observation, and monitoring the program. This engagement not only helps community members further develop literacy, numeracy, and functional literacy, but promotes critical awareness of the socioeconomic conditions of indigenous peoples. Young (2002, p. 231) argues that such a locally grounded approach in the Philippines is necessary for "empowerment, equipping students for lifelong learning."

Mohanty, Mishra, Reddy, and Ramesh (2009) critique India tribal children's disadvantage in education and society due to language hierarchies and discuss the role of tribal communities and their funds of knowledge in creation and implementation of a mother tongue-based multilingual education policy for tribal children living in Andhra Pradesh and Orissa. Andhra Pradesh has introduced eight and Orissa ten tribal languages into the public schools. In collaboration with teachers, tribal communities, community leaders, and local writers and artists, the multilingual education programs in these states have incorporated tribal knowledge and cultural practices into their curriculum, textbooks, and teaching materials. The level of competencies in different curricular areas such as mathematics and language is based on cultural themes. Songs, games, and other culture-specific activities are used to teach numeracy and literacy skills. The sequencing of such materials depends on the village calendar that is based on seasonal community activities, festivals, and special events (Mohanty et al., 2009). Tribal children are given opportunities to participate in community events to ensure social and cultural interaction in their home languages. Most teachers are recruited from the local community and, thus, play a critical role in developing textbooks and teaching-learning materials.

The aforementioned community-based efforts are geared toward creating new histories and new consciousness about what counts as legitimate knowledge, language, and pedagogies (Hough et al., 2009; Smith, 2012). This new consciousness emerges from collaboration and critical dialogue among teachers, parents, students, policy makers, and experts toward understanding the existing linguistic, cultural, and educational realities and creating alternative practices that best fit local ecology and knowledge. This consciousness is built on indigenous and ethnic minoritized people's counter-narratives (Crump, 2014; Delgado, 1989; Montecinos, 1995), which challenge dominant narratives of language education, epistemology, and literacy practices. Adopting a counter-narrative approach, McCarty, Romero, and Zepeda (2006) also engage Native American indigenous youth in analyzing and becoming aware of the marginalizing impact of dominant language ideologies and policies. Building on their own personal, familial, and community life experiences, youth enter into dialogue through which they develop awareness of power relations and take activist positions toward caring about and creating space for indigenous languages in education.

Community/parental engagement is an essential component for students' educational achievement (Arias, 2015; García & Kleifgen, 2010). However, the existing mainstream education system, which gives more emphasis on standard language and standardized testing, lacks effective policies and plans for school-community engagement. Arias (2015) discusses the importance of community/parental engagement in addressing immigrant and language minoritized children's linguistic and academic needs. While arguing the need for parental engagement in supporting minoritized students' educational success, Arias urges us to focus on (at least) "a two-day dialogue" between school and parents/communities toward recognizing their linguistic and cultural values and strengths as resources for learning. While critiquing the dominant discourse of "a cultural deficit model," Arias argues that the cultural values of immigrant communities in education contribute to addressing low educational achievement among minoritized children. Therefore, she argues that schools need to

> [i]dentify and recognize the cultural and educational strengths of marginalized families, while realizing that parents may not have the social currency/capital to negotiate the unfamiliar terrain of the schools. Immigrant parents often experience confusion and frustration with an educational system that not only misunderstand their cultural values and beliefs, but also places additional barriers that impede their full involvement in their children's schooling.
>
> (p. 286)

For effective parent/community engagement, there is a need for an ideological shift in redefining the role and identity of parents/communities in education. As Arias (2015) maintains, schools should consider parents as "co-designers and active participants" in decision-making processes about their children's education. Such a reconsideration could encourage parents to take ownership of school-related activities that eventually contribute to "improving student's overall persistence in school and academic achievement" (Arias, 2015, p. 288). Giving an example of how a non-profit organization, *Parents Involvement in Quality Education*, has engaged "low-income" and "limited-English-speaking" families to support school success, Arias (2015) provides four major goals of parent/community engaged in the decision-making process. These goals include (1) empowering parents to be teachers of their children; (2) connecting low-income parents with their community schools; (3) increasing home–school communication and collaboration; and (4) establishing an effective home/school-support team. Focus on these goals embraces voice and agency of parents and helps schools to raise awareness of how funds of knowledge embedded in cultural and linguistic practices are important for children's success in school.

Chávez-Reyes (2012) promotes inclusive, collaborative, and long-term parent engagement toward improving the academic success of minoritized students and English language learners. In analyzing how the US mainstream education policies have unrecognized the role of parents and community in education, she claims that an inclusive approach to parent–community engagement is necessary to address growing multilingual and multicultural diversity. Ideological awareness is crucial to ensuring parent–/community–school engagement. As Chávez-Reyes (2012) argues, teachers and schools must "*accept* and *value* the language and culture of immigrant families and their children to authentically interact and collaborate with parents" (p. 475). In addition, schools need to *acknowledge* unequal power relations between schools and parents and seek the means to *empower* parents to work together with schools toward academic success of all English language learners (Chávez-Reyes, 2012). However, she contends that the existing approach to parent/community engagement toward improving students' tests scores to attain federal and state funding dictates parents "to behave in particular ways" (Chavez-Reyes, 2012, p. 475); it does not necessarily address power inequalities between schools and parents nor provide relevant curricula for minoritized students. Therefore, it is necessary to lobby for inclusive approaches that "emphasize human relations, cultivation of interpersonal relationships, and organizational functioning to improve circumstances for ELLs' academic performance and development" (Chavez-Reyes, 2012, p. 476). The inclusive approach to parent–school engagement focuses not only on "participation" but on "empowerment" of parents/families to take an active role in their children's learning process by utilizing their own linguistic and cultural resources toward effective education. Rockwell, Andre, and Hawley (2010) argue that

> [e]mpowerment is not an "add it on later" idea but an important element in planning parent involvement opportunities especially for families that are considered at risk, are poor, belong to a minority racial group or have non-mainstream culture and language…empowerment is one of the keys to overcoming social class and cultural barriers as they relate to involvement in schools.
>
> (p. 329)

Scholars have proposed various strategies for parent/community engagement. Family visits, community outreach, and creation and implementation of multilingual and multicultural policies are some of the major strategies (Chávez-Reyes, 2012; Souto-Manning & Swick, 2006). At the center of all these strategies lies ideological clarification among schools, teachers, and policy makers with regard to what counts as effective educational policies and practices for minoritized children and multilingual learners. Most important, parents should be considered a source of knowledge and given space to create and implement multilingual and multicultural policies.

García and Kleifgen (2010) have further built on "ecologies of parental engagement" (Barton, Drake, Perez, St. Louis, & George, 2004) that emphasize parent/community engagement in educating emergent bilingual children. The ecologies of parental engagement approach go beyond the traditional notion of parent/community involvement and "takes into account the different styles of action taken by parents [communities] from diverse ethnolinguistic backgrounds" (García & Kleifgen, 2010, p. 100). This implies that schools and teachers need a deeper ethnographic understanding of the values and epistemologies of diverse sociocultural and sociolinguistic groups. In other words, as students' ways of knowing, doing, and being are shaped by their cultural, linguistic, and economic backgrounds, schools and teachers are called to promote policies and practices that embrace the broad spectrum and in-depth nature of community "funds of knowledge" as resources (González, Moll, & Amanti, 2005). Espinoza-Herrold's study (2007, p. 263) also shows that funds of knowledge "can be interpreted as 'engaged participation'; they are not static but, rather, can be redefined, interpreted, and applied to variable contexts of participation."

The studies mentioned above reveal that parent/community engagement is "a shared responsibility" (García & Kleifgen, 2010) in which both school and community develop linguistically and culturally responsive policies and practices. Given that multilingual learners have diverse ways of speaking and learning, it is further important to provide equal space for all of the student home languages in school. This requires schools, teachers, and policy makers to rethink education from a multilingual and multicultural perspective rather than from a standard language and standardized testing perspective. Scholars such as Zentella (2005) and Faltis (2006) have shown that the existing educational policies and approaches to parent/community engagement blame the minoritized and low-income parents as people who are "disinterested" in their children's education. However, these scholars contend that the existing policies and approaches are faulty in that they fail to take into account the ways in which different linguistic and cultural groups engage in educating their children. In other words, the existing system lacks appropriate policies to recognize and capitalize on community linguistic and cultural resources as integral to quality education. Gold, Simon, and Brown's study (2002, as cited in García & Kleifgen, 2010) further shows that schools and policy makers need to go beyond monolingual and monocultural deficit views of education and collaborate with community-based grassroots organizations for effective parent/community engagement. Because different communities self-organize to support their children's education, schools and teachers need to work with such organizations to create an inclusive school space in terms of language, culture, and identity.

Tenery (2005) provides insight into understanding how teachers and schools can ensure parent/community engagement in children's education. This study shows that it is necessary for teachers to have a deeper understanding and awareness of students' linguistic and cultural practices. For Tenery (2005), home visits can help teachers to understand familial survival strategies, domains of knowledge, and language and cultural practices. Furthermore, home visits can establish strong parent–school relationships and trust and provide teachers with a rich understanding of their students. This kind of engaged practice supports the voices, knowledge, values, and identities of children and communities from diverse linguistic backgrounds. Together, the studies mentioned above imply a paradigm shift toward addressing sociopolitical, linguistic, and cultural inequalities in education. This shift considers parents/communities and their languages, values, and identities central to ensuring an inclusive and effective education for all students. These studies further indicate that schools and policy makers should go beyond the existing narrow ideology of education as acquisition of standard languages through traditional means and toward language education awareness and community involvement.

In sum, studies across countries and territories show that ensuring multilingual education policies and practices helps to alleviate poverty, social exclusion, and/or marginalization of language communities. Skutnabb-Kangas and Heugh (2012) argue that lack of multilingual education for minoritized children contributes to educational failure and perpetuation of poverty. While critiquing the erasure of minoritized languages in school as one of the major factors for social exclusion of indigenous and ethnic minoritized people, Skutnabb-Kangas and Heugh (2012) claim that multilingual education supports sustainable local development; contributes to preservation of local ecology; and increases access of all children to wider education and economic resources worldwide. Besides the foregoing efforts to support home language education, Benson, Heugh, Bogale, and Yohannes (2012) show that the use of children's "mother tongue" up to the eighth grade of schooling contributes tremendously to increased academic achievement of ethnic minoritized children in Ethiopia. Studies from counties such as Bolivia (e.g., Hornberger & Swinehart, 2012; López, 2006), Cambodia, Ethiopia, and Mozambique (e.g., Benson, 2010), Papua New Guinea (e.g., Pickford, 2005), Vietnam and Thailand (e.g., Kosonen & Young 2009), and Timor-Leste (e.g., Taylor-Leech, 2013) show that ensuring the use of children's home languages, indigenous epistemologies, and cultural values not only promotes equitable multilingual education but can support community members, teachers, and students toward social transformation.

Conclusions: Engaged Language Policies and Practices

In recognizing the recent call for explicit denouncement and denaturalization of hegemonic language ideologies and practices (Flores & Rosa, 2015; Tupas, 2015), this chapter has focused on multiple methods, projects, strategies, and pedagogies that are transformative and informed by multilingual ideologies, indigenous epistemologies, and culturally appropriate education. This chapter aimed to portray the process of language policy engagement toward challenging "monolingual habitus" (Benson, 2013; Gogolin, 1997) and re-imagining equitable multilingual education policies and practices. As discussed in this chapter, an equitable multilingual policy rejects language hierarchies, unequal privileging of languages, and monoglossic ideologies (García, 2009; May, 2014). In acknowledging the complexity of multilingualism and multilingual policies and practices, we have revealed processes of engaged language policy-making across a range of sociopolitical contexts.

While portraying the importance of translanguaging in multilingual education policy from the bottom up, we have further argued that this approach is not just a pedagogical set of methods for teaching multiliteracies and multiple languages but, most importantly, is intended to promote creative, critical, and transformative language policies (García & Li, 2014). It is creative in that it engages multilingual learners in flouting normative boundaries and rules by using their existing language knowledge. It is critical because it challenges a one-language-only ideology and the traditional view of multilingualism as the sum total of multiple autonomous languages. It is transformative because it builds on students' real linguistic, cultural, and sociopolitical experiences. As we discussed in this chapter, translanguaging embraces children's home languages as resources not only for learning academic content but for engaging multilingual learners in the process of ideological becoming (Bakhtin, 1981). As a practice-based policy, translanguaging provides multilingual learners a dialogic space in which they bring their histories, ideologies, identities, and voices into language education and policy discussion. Through this process, multilingual learners engage in negotiating the tension between dominant and counterpublic discourses and ideologies. Furthermore, translanguaging helps multilingual learners to become aware of linguistic, historical, and cultural inequalities and empowers them to take activist positions toward social transformation.

As Howard Adams (1995), an indigenous Métis scholar and activist, argues, the policies and practices discussed represent "counter-consciousness," that is, critical awareness of marginalization. Alternative policies that lead to agency and activism have the power to transform hegemonic nation-state, neoliberal, and standard language ideologies. This counter-consciousness in language policy emerges from engaging teachers, students, communities, and parents toward explicit discussion of sociopolitical issues that are embedded in their lived experience as well as in dominant practices. In other words, we have argued that multilingual education should be understood not just as learning multiple languages; rather, it should be taken as a "translanguaging space" (Li, 2011a) in which multilingual children, parents, and ethnic minoritized communities feel safe to share their struggles, histories, and knowledge toward becoming aware of what counts as a legitimate language policy and practice for their own empowerment. Cummins (2006) sums up an equitable education policy as one in which multilingual learners' agency and knowledge are recognized toward providing opportunities for identity investment and multilingual expertise.

We have also shown that an equitable multilingual policy embraces a *pedagogy of the possible* (Hélot & O'Laoire, 2011) and a *pedagogy of hope* (Freire, 1992), both of which seek critical awareness among teachers, parents, policy makers, and students of the educational, cognitive, and sociopolitical challenges and possibilities of multilingualism. At the center of these pedagogies are community *engagement* and local funds of knowledge. We have argued that drawing communities of families, educators, and advocates into dialogic engagement grounded in collaborative actions provides insights into understanding ways in which equitable policy is created and maintained. In sum, we have shown that reimagining language policy from a multilingual perspective requires ideological awareness that builds on the ideological becoming of parents, teachers, students, experts, and policy makers.

6
AFTERWORD
Language Policy Rights and Resources

In the 1990s, Henri Lefebvre conceptualized "the right to the city" as a means toward addressing growing disenfranchisement among those affected by harmful liberal and neoliberal ideologies that inform social policies (1991, 1996). Purcell (2002) specifically holds that this concept involves "a radical restructuring of social, political, and economic relations, both in the city and beyond" (p. 101). Piller (2016) further addresses the need for the right to languages in stating that "...if we do not understand how linguistic diversity intersects with social justice and if we are unable to even recognize disadvantage and discrimination on the basis of language, we will not be able to work toward positive change" (p. 5). Thus, we call for "the right to language policy," which questions liberal/neoliberal assumptions behind policies and emphasizes participatory approaches in language policy-making processes. In taking a transformative perspective, we more specifically hold that the right to language policy-making calls for alternative ideologies and practices that resist and alter existing neoliberal structuring. In other words, engaged language policy reimagines new strategies for resisting neoliberal globalization and seeks to enfranchise the disenfranchised.

The right to language policy is concerned mainly with meaningful participation of people who are impacted by inequitable and/or insufficient language policies. Our contention is that liberal and neoliberal ideologies often constrain the right of education in one's mother tongue and other accessible languages. Scholars and educators are increasingly called on to address linguistic inequalities among people who are affected by linguistic oppression through providing for the right to create and recreate policy (see Ramanathan, 2013; Tupas, 2015). In other words, meaningful language policy transformation is possible only by ensuring the right of the disenfranchised and marginalized to engage in the process of policy creation and implementation. While we acknowledge the liberal ideology of language rights, we hold that this approach alone is insufficient for resisting and transforming marginalizing nation-state and neoliberal ideologies. We summarize here key themes that emerged through our historical, ideological and inquiry based analyses toward identifying the means by which equitable policies and practices are achieved.

1. *Engaging in humanitarian language education welfare involves empowerment of the disenfranchised toward denaturalizing and then transforming harmful ideologies.* This necessitates engaging participants in critical analysis of both public sphere (Habermas, 1985, 1989) and counter-public sphere ideologies (Fraser, 1990; Warner, 2002). Piller (2016) reveals that discourses on linguistic diversity often "contribute to injustice precisely by concealing inequality at the same time that they create inequality by marking one group as 'normal' and the other as 'diverse'" (pp. 19–20). In response, we promote language policy inquiry that focuses on "awakening a sense of injustice" (Stoudt et al., 2011) among all participants—educators, students, parents, community members—through exploring and analyzing hegemonic language ideologies that limit the use of minoritized languages in public spheres. Also, rather than viewing language-policy-as-product, we emphasize language-policy-as-process that seeks to involve all concerned toward social justice, which critical philosopher Nancy Fraser defines as "parity of participation" (Fraser, 2005). While ideological analyses inform the politics of local, national, and global policies, documentation of the processes involved in establishing equitable policies provides models of equitable and effective language policies and plans. We specifically explore and describe ways in which *engaged language policy and practices* (ELP) works as an all-inclusive community of forward-looking participants dedicated to innovative and collective exploration of policies, plans, and practices that best serve their needs. It is, moreover, a common rather than an individual right since this transformation inevitably depends on the exercise of collective power to reshape the processes of language policy formation and implementation.

2. *Engaged language policy perspectives call for decolonizing language ideologies that support hegemonic nation-states and neoliberal language policies* (Lin & Martin, 2005). Indigenous peoples' languages are often most threatened given a perceived lack of utility of these languages in the wider social and linguistic market place. Thus, we argue for transformative processes of decolonization that "engages with imperialism and colonialism at multiple levels" and involves "a more critical understanding of the underlying assumptions, motivations and values which inform research practices" (Smith, 1999, p. 20). In exposing marginalizing language ideologies, we seek to promote alternative policies, ideologies, and practices toward indigenous and

language minoritized social justice (Conteh & Meier, 2014; Slaughter & Hajek, 2015; Tupas, 2015).

While acknowledging that language procedures, discourses, and practices are influenced by hegemonic policies, we hold that neoliberal ideologies consequently often promote linguistic hierarchy, unequal distribution of resources, and subsequent disenfranchisement of those who lack access to socioeconomic and political power. In response, our ELP perspective goes beyond resistance toward building alternative language policy ideologies and practices. Lin (2013) further supports the view that liberatory engaged approaches can counter claims of language policy as homogenous, autonomous and, subsequently, a "standardized" prepackaged commodity. Instead, we argue that engaged language policy research focuses on grassroots, fluid, and dynamic language practices that promote educational success through collaborative school and community action. Smith (2012) further argues that policy-making should not completely reject dominant language ideologies but rather be understood as "processes which connect, inform and clarify the tensions between the local, the regional and the global" (p. 39). Thus, we emphasize that language policy actors, such as teachers, students, and parents/community, are called on to engage in collaborative exploration and dialogue toward clarifying and resisting marginalizing ideologies. We further support language policy actors in endeavors to identify ideological tensions while building agency and activism toward actions for change.

3. *An engaged perspective considers linguistic diversity from a critical standpoint that takes an egalitarian view that knows no boundaries or barriers to language policies and practices.* This approach promotes critical awareness of how dominant discourses either intrude on multilingual practices or support linguistic diversity that counters language injustices. The engaged approach discussed in this book calls for shifting our attention from concealing social inequalities towards finding ways to recognize the value of linguistic diversity. This process requires us to engage educators, students, parents, and community member in language policy inquiry that focuses on "awakening a sense of injustice" (Stoudt et al., 2011). Studies such as those by Stoudt et al. (2011) and Piller (2016) have shown that use of minoritized languages is commonly restricted even when constitutional and legal provisions guarantee the right to use one's "mother tongue" in education and other public spheres. The right to language policy challenges token representation of marginalized peoples in the process of policy creation while arguing for recognition of local knowledge and rights toward transforming inequitable top-down language policies. Our engaged approach emerges from our close reading of language policy discourses

and practices from around the globe and our own experiences working with minoritized populations.

We have specifically argued that policy scholars are called to address the means by which marginalized communities are empowered to engage in full participation at every stage of language policy creation and implementation. Drawing from Freire's dialogic process of conscientization, ELP aims to raise consciousness among all the various actors involved in policy decision making toward engagement in countering unjust practices. The transglobal cases we provide represent on-the-ground work in differing states of addressing conscientization, resistance, and/or transformation. We further emphasize critical ethnography as embedded in ELP as means for gaining understanding of participants' personal experience of history, place, and culture in relation to globalization, neoliberalism, and nationalism. We also promote studies that provide exemplar equitable practices toward ELP that portray the processes involved in mutual engagement and resistance toward realizing equity and human welfare. We feel that, as language and social equity advocates, further ELP theoretical conceptualization and social practices portrayal are important in realizing social justice.

4. *A pedagogy of the possible approach engages teachers, parents, students, and other concerned language policy actors in contesting hegemonic ideologies.* Hélot and O'Laoire (2011) call for inviting teachers and learners to respond to all possibilities and potentialities of multilingual classrooms. A pedagogy of the possible builds on critical awareness among teachers, students, parents, and others concerned about sociopolitical inequalities, marginalizing ideologies, and their own agency and activism toward transforming hegemonic ideologies and practices. A pedagogy of the possible further rejects marginalizing nation-state ideology and embraces local multilingualism and cultures as resources for education. We specifically argue for grounding collective analyses in awareness of macro-level ideologies and imposed policies and practices that are detrimental to human and educational welfare. In promoting awareness, we emphasize the need for researchers/community facilitators to take seriously their position as learner and advocate in dialogue with others as key participants in the engaged process. We have specifically suggested placing those directly involved, such as students, parents, and community members, at the center of emancipatory processes. Tollefson (2013) emphasizes that "members of communities which programs they seek to serve must be able to design and implement the programs" (p. 305). He further argues that "…commitments to language maintenance and revitalization can rarely be imposed successfully by policy makers seeking top-down implementation of their programs" (p. 307). We further suggest that reimagining language policy from a multilingual perspective requires extensive and intensive dialogue toward ideological becoming of parents,

teachers, students, experts, and policy makers that collectively inform multilingual activism and advocacy.
5. *Multilingual learners' "identity texts" and "identity investment" as described by Cummins (2005, 2006) as well as García and Leiva's (2014) translanguaging as a mechanism for social justice provide important insights into engaging policy makers, teachers, and parents in creating transformative space for linguistic diversity in the face of increased English language dominance in education worldwide.* Cummins (2006) argues that policy makers and educators must first and foremost create pedagogical and interpersonal space for multilingual learners' *identity investment* that greatly affects cognitive engagement in learning processes. This perspective reimagines multilingual policies and practices that recognize students' knowledge of home languages and literacy skills as resource for cognitively engaged and transformative learning processes. Such policies provide students with opportunities to negotiate and invest their identities in classrooms and engage them in critical and situated dialogue to understand socio-political power relations toward constructing positive self-images.
6. *While various approaches to equitable language education described here hold promise for schools and communities to provide equitable education for linguistic minorities, many sites and circumstances dictate more aggressive, inclusive, and comprehensive approaches to meeting the needs of marginalized student populations.* Studies across countries and territories show that ensuring multilingual education policies and practices help to alleviate poverty, social exclusion, and/or marginalization of language communities. Skutnabb-Kangas and Heugh (2012) argue that lack of multilingual education for minoritized children contributes to educational failure and perpetuation of poverty. While critiquing the erasure of minoritized languages in school as one of the major factors for social exclusion of indigenous and ethnic minoritized people, Skutnabb-Kangas and Heugh (2012) claim that multilingual education supports sustainable local development, contributes to preservation of local ecology, and increases access of all children to wider education and economic resources world-wide.

Gandin and Apple's (2002) model of a Citizen School in Brazil supports egalitarian and transformative education. This school offers marginalized working class students the opportunity to realize effective community-based schooling. The Citizen School recognizes the right of subaltern populations to develop educational policies that address their specific needs. Thus, the school upholds a strong ideological position of democratized education by challenging hegemonic neoliberal school policies and practices. Gandin and Apple (2002) specifically point out the importance of democratic engagement in setting up goals for transformative pedagogies of practice. Towards these ends, the Citizen School involves parents, students, and teachers in collective decision-making in recognizing the identities, knowledge, and voices of socio-politically and economically marginalized communities. Our book takes on this engaged model in supporting alternative schooling policies and practices across communities towards ensuring marginalized people's parity of participation (Fraser, 2008). Engaged language policy and practices more specifically reimagine alternative ideologies, epistemologies, and models for implementing non-standard and fluid multilingual practices that support minoritized communities, educators, parents, and students in realizing transformative education and welfare across public spheres (see Ramanathan, 2013). Tollefson (2013) further argues that

> …the alternative to repressive language policies is democratic pluralism, which means establishing and supporting institutions, regulations, and decision-making systems and practices that ensure the widest possible participation in policy-making by all social, economic, cultural, and linguistic groups. Extending democratic pluralism involves seeking an end to discrimination based on ascribed categories such as language and ethnicity, and finding ways to ensure that individuals and groups who are affected by policies have direct involvement and power in policy-making. (pp. 308)

This position reflects our own stance on democratic pluralism and hope that our engaged language policy and practices approach will help further inclusive, collaborative, and meaningful activism toward collective equality and justice.

7. *Our engaged language policy perspective calls for rejecting neoliberal-driven policies and promoting equity of voice toward equitable policies.* As scholars such as Conteh and Meier (2014), Tupas (2015), and Hajek and Slaughter (2015) argue, exposing discriminatory and hegemonic language ideologies is the first step toward transforming language policies. At the same time, our ELP perspective goes beyond a resistance paradigm and focuses on building alternative ideologies and a knowledge base for equitable language policies. Lin (2013) argues that this perspective engages language policy actors in "breaking hegemonic knowledge claims" that consider language a homogenous and autonomous entity and "standardized" prepacked market commodity. We hold that language policy should focus more on grassroots fluid and dynamic language practices in order to bridge an increased equity gap in schools and communities.

8. *Alternative language ideologies and practices reimagine equitable language policies that build on local sociopolitical/historical reality and epistemologies.* Gegeo and Watson-Gegeo (2002, 2013) model engaged language policy that builds on critical indigenous praxis and indigenous epistemology. In other words, we argue that the focus should concern people's own critical reflection on their cultural, historical, sociopolitical, and economic conditions. Rather than

focusing on standardized knowledge and language practices, our engaged language policy pays attention to how people from different cultural and social groups create and formulate knowledge while participating in libratory discourse. In other words, the construction of an alternative knowledge base for language policy emerges from critical reflection on local history, culture, place, and values. Therefore, we argue for shifting our attention away from nation-state, standard language, and commodification and toward counter-histories, counter-narratives, and counter-discourses (e.g., Lee, 2009; McCarty, Zepeda, & Romero, 2006). This shift recognizes histories of linguistic oppression and struggles in reclaiming marginalized voices and identities as resources for reimagining equitable language policy and practices. We have centrally argued for the need to draw on a repertoire of past, current, and future language policy endeavors toward articulating a new and inclusive approach to language policy and practices. Toward these ends, we recognize past and current influences on community and school use of home languages while arguing for self-determination as the means by which communities and scholars support the legitimacy of situated language practices. We look forward to ongoing dialogue with all concerned toward engaging the challenges and potential for equitable language policies and practices that are wholly committed to human welfare.

REFERENCES

Achugar, M. (2015). Critical language awareness approaches in the Americas: Theoretical principles, pedagogical practices and distribution of intellectual labor. *Linguistics and Education, 32,* 1–4.
Adams, H. (1995). *A tortured people: The politics of colonization.* Penticton, BC: Theytus Books.
Akindes, F. Y. (2001). Sudden rush: *Na Mele Paleoleo* (Hawaiian Rap) as liberatory discourse. *Discourse, 23*(1), 82–98.
Alim, H. S. (2011). Global ill-literacies: Hip hop cultures, youth identities, and the politics of literacy. *Review of Research in Education, 35*(1), 120–146.
Alim, H. S., Ibrahim, A., & Pennycook, A. (Eds.) (2009). *Global linguistic flows: Hip-hop cultures, youth identities, and the politics of language.* New York: Routledge.
Alimi, M. M. (2016). Micro language planning and cultural renaissance in Botswana. *Language Policy, 15*(1) 49–69.
Althusser, L. (1971). *Lenin and philosophy and other essays* (trans. B. Brewster). London: New Left Books.
Anderson, B. (1991). *Imagined communities: Reflections on the origin and spread of nationalism.* London: Verso.
Annamalai, E. (2003). Reflections on a language policy for multilingualism. *Language Policy, 2*(2), 113–132.
Annamalai, E. (2013). India's economic restructuring with English: Benefits and costs. In J. W. Tollefson (Ed.), *Language policies in education: Critical issues* (2nd ed.) (pp. 191–208). New York: Routledge.
Anzaldúa, G. (1987). *Borderlands/La Frontera: The new mestiza.* San Francisco, CA: Aunt Lute Books.
Appadurai, A. (1996). *Modernity al large: Cultural dimensions of globalization.* Minneapolis, MN: University of Minnesota Press.
Appadurai, A. (2006). The right to research. *Globalization, Societies, and Education, 4*(2), 167–177.

Apple, M. W. (1989). How equality has been redefined in the conservative restoration. In W. G. Secada (Ed.), *Equity in education* (pp. 7–25). New York: Falmer Press.
Apple, M. W. (2001). Comparing neo-liberal projects and inequality in education. *Comparative Education*, *37*(4), 409–423.
Archer, L., Francis, B., & Mau, A. (2009). 'Boring and stressful' or 'ideal' learning spaces? Pupils' constructions of teaching and learning in Chinese supplementary schools. *Research Papers in Education*, *24*(4), 477–497.
Arias, M. B. (2015). Parent and community involvement in bilingual and multilingual education. In W. E. Wright, S. Boun, & O. García (Eds.), *The handbook of bilingual and multilingual education* (pp. 282–298). Malden, MA: Wiley Blackwell.
Awasthi, L. D. (2008). Importation of ideologies from Macaulay Minutes to Wood Commission. *Journal of Education and Research*, *1*, 21–30.
Bailey, B. (2012). Heteroglossia. In M. Martin-Jones, A. Blackledge, & A. Creese (Eds.), *The Routledge handbook of multilingualism* (pp. 499–507). Abingdon: Routledge.
Baker, C. (2011). *Foundations of bilingual education and bilingualism* (5th ed.). Bristol: Multilingual Matters.
Bakhtin, M. M. (1981). *The dialogical imagination: Fours essays*. Austin, TX: University of Texas Press.
Bakhtin, M. M. (1984). *Rabelais and his world* (vol. 341). Bloomington, IN: Indiana University Press.
Bale, J. (2015). Language policy and global political economy. In T. Ricento (Ed.), *Language and political economy: English in a global context* (pp. 72–96). Oxford: Oxford University Press.
Ball, A. F. (2000a). Preparing teachers for diversity: Lessons learned from the US and South Africa. *Teaching and Teacher Education*, *16*(4), 491–509.
Ball, A. F. (2000b). Empowering pedagogies that enhance the learning of multicultural students. *Teachers College Record*, *102*(6), 1006–1034.
Ball, J. (2010). *Enhancing learning of children from diverse language backgrounds: Mother tongue-based bilingual or multilingual education in early childhood and early primary school years*. Retrieved from http://eyeonkids.ca/docs/files/unesco_mother-tongue_based_ey_2010.pdf.
Barton, A. C., Drake, C., Perez, J. G., St. Louis, K. S., & George, M. (2004). Ecologies of parental engagement in urban education. *Educational Researcher*, *33*(4), 3–12.
Benson, C. (2005). *Girls, educational equity and mother tongue-based teaching*. Bangkok: UNESCO Bangkok. Retrieved from www2.unescobkk.org/elib/publications/Girls_Edu_Equity/index.htm.
Benson, C. (2010). How multilingual African contexts are pushing educational research and practice in new directions. *Language and Education*, *24*(4), 323–336.
Benson, C. (2013). Towards adopting a multilingual habitus in educational development. In C. Benson & K. Kosonen (Eds.), *Language issues in comparative education: Inclusive teaching and learning in non-dominant languages and cultures* (pp. 283–299). Rotterdam: Sense Publishers.
Benson, C., Heugh, K., Bogale, B., & Yohannes, M. A. G. (2012). Multilingual education in Ethiopian primary schools. In T. Skutnabb-Kangas & K. Heugh (Eds.), *Multilingual education and sustainable diversity work: From periphery to center* (pp. 32–61). Abingdon: Routledge.
Bhabha, H. K. (1991). *Nation and narration*. London: Routledge.
Bhabha, H. K. (1994). *The location of culture*. New York: Routledge.

Blackledge, A., & Creese, A. (2010). *Multilingualism: A critical perspective*. London: Continuum.
Blackledge, A., & Creese, A. (Eds.) (2014). *Heteroglossia as practice and pedagogy*. Heidelberg: Springer.
Block, D. (2006). *Multilingual identities in a global city: London stories*. London: Palgrave.
Block, D. (2007). The rise of identity in SLA research, post Firth and Wagner (1997). *The Modern Language Journal, 91*(s1), 863–876.
Block, D. (2014). *Social class in applied linguistics*. New York: Routledge.
Block, D., Gray, J., & Holborow, M. (2012). *Neoliberalism and applied linguistics*. New York: Routledge.
Blommaert, J. (1991). How much culture is there in intercultural communication? In J. Blommaert & J. Verschueren (Eds.), *The pragmatics of intercultural and international communication* (pp. 13–31). Amsterdam: Benjamins.
Blommaert, J. (Ed.) (1999). *Language ideological debates*. Berlin: Mouton de Gruyter.
Blommaert, J. (2005). *Discourse: A critical introduction*. Cambridge: Cambridge University Press.
Blommaert, J. (2006). Language policy and national identity. In T. Ricento (Ed.), *An introduction to language policy: Theory and method* (pp. 238–254). Malden, MA: Blackwell.
Blommaert, J. (2008). Notes of power. *Working Papers in Language Diversity, 7*, 2–5.
Blommaert, J. (2009). Ethnography and democracy: Hymes' political theory of language. *Text & Talk, 29*(3), 257–276.
Blommaert, J. (2010). *The sociolinguistics of globalization*. Cambridge: Cambridge University Press.
Blommaert, J. (2013). Policy, policing and the ecology of social norms: Ethnographic monitoring revisited. *International Journal of the Sociology of Language, 219*, 123–140.
Blommaert, J. (2014). *State ideology and language in Tanzania* (2nd ed.). Edinburgh: Edinburgh University Press.
Blommaert, J., & Rampton, B. (2011). Language and superdiversity. *Diversities, 13*(2), 3–21.
Blommaert, J., & Verschueren, J. (1998). The role of language in European nationalist ideologies. *Pragmatics, 2*(3), 355–375.
Bourdieu, P. (1984). *Distinction: A social critique of the judgement of taste*. Cambridge, MA: Harvard University Press.
Bourdieu, P. (1991). *Language and symbolic power*. Cambridge: Polity Press.
Brown, E. R. (2007). The quiet disaster of No Child Left Behind. In K. J. Saltman (Ed.), *Schooling and the politics of disaster* (pp. 123–140). New York: Routledge.
Burkett, M. (2011). In search of refuge: Pacific islands, climate-induced migration, and the legal frontier. *Asia Pacific Issues, 98*, 1–8.
Cammarota, J., & Fine, M. (Eds.) (2008). *Revolutionizing education: Youth participatory action research in motion*. Abingdon: Routledge.
Canagarajah, A. S. (1999). *Resisting linguistic imperialism in English teaching*. Oxford: Oxford University Press.
Canagarajah, A. S. (Ed.) (2005). *Reclaiming the local in language policy and practice*. Mahwah, NJ: Lawrence Erlbaum.
Canagarajah, S. (2006). Ethnographic methods in language policy. In T. Ricento (Ed.), *An introduction to language policy: Theory and method* (pp. 153–169). Malden, MA: Blackwell Publishing.
Canagarajah, S., & Ashraf, H. (2013). Multilingualism and education in South Asia: Resolving policy/practice dilemmas. *Annual Review of Applied Linguistics, 33*, 258–285.

Carney, S. (2003). Globalization, neo-liberalism and the limitations of school effectiveness research in developing countries: The case of Nepal. *Globalization, Societies and Education, 1*(1), 87–101.

Cazden, C. B., John, V. P., & Hymes, D. (Eds.) (1972). *Functions of language in the classroom*. New York: Teachers College Press.

Central Bureau of Statistics (2011). *National living standards survey 2010–2011*. Kathmandu: Government of Nepal.

Chávez-Reyes, C. (2012). Engaging in critical social dialogue with socially diverse undergraduate teacher candidates at a California State University. *Teacher Education Quarterly, 39*(2), 43–62.

Clair, R. P. (2012). Engaged ethnography and the story(ies) of the anti-sweatshop movement. *Cultural Studies <=> Critical Methodologies, 12*(2), 132–145.

Clark, R., & Ivanic, R. (1992). Consciousness-raising about the writing process. In C. James & P. Garrett (Eds.), *Language awareness in the classroom* (pp. 168–185). London: Longman.

Clarke, K. M. (2010). Toward a critically engaged ethnographic practice. *Current Anthropology, 51*(2), 301–312.

Clifford, J., & Marcus, G. (1986). *Writing culture: The poetics and politics of ethnography*. Berkeley, CA: University of California Press.

Coelho, F. O., & Henze, R. (2014). English for what? Rural Nicaraguan teachers' local responses to national educational policy. *Language Policy, 13*(2), 145–163.

Coleman, H. (2011). Developing countries and the English language: Rhetoric, risks, roles and recommendations. In H. Coleman (Ed.), *Dreams and realities: Developing countries and the English language* (pp. 9–21). London: British Council.

Conteh, J., & Meier, G. (Eds.) (2014). *The multilingual turn in languages education: Opportunities and challenges*. Bristol: Multilingual Matters.

Cook, V. J. (1991). The poverty-of-the-stimulus argument and multi-competence. *Second Language Research, 7*(2), 103–117.

Corson, D. (1999). *Language policy in schools*. London: Lawrence Erlbaum.

Coupland, N. (2007). *Style: Language variation and identity*. Cambridge: Cambridge University Press.

Creese, A., & Blackledge, A. (2010). Translanguaging in the bilingual classroom: A pedagogy for learning and teaching? *The Modern Language Journal, 94*(1), 103–115.

Creese, A., & Martin, P. (2008). Classroom ecologies: A case study from a Gujarati complementary school in England. In *Encyclopedia of language and education* (pp. 3142–3151). Berlin: Springer.

Creese, A., Bhatt, A., Bhojani, N., & Martin, P. (2008). Fieldnotes in team ethnography: Researching complementary schools. *Qualitative Research, 8*(2), 197–215.

Crump, A. (2014). Introducing LangCrit: Critical language and race theory. *Critical Inquiry in Language Studies, 11*(3), 207–224.

Cummins, J. (2005). A proposal for action: Strategies for recognizing heritage language competence as a learning resource within the mainstream classroom. *Modern Language Journal, 89*(4), 585–592.

Cummins, J. (2006). Identity texts: The imaginative construction of self through multiliteracy pedagogy. In O. García, T. Skutnabb-Kangas, & M. E. Torres-Guzmán (Eds.), *Imagining multilingual schools: Languages in education and glocalization* (pp. 51–68). Clevedon: Multilingual Matters.

Cummins, J. (2007). Rethinking monolingual instructional strategies in multilingual classrooms. *Canadian Journal of Applied Linguistics/Revue canadienne de linguistique appliquée*, *10*(2), 221–240.

Cummins, J., & Early, M. (2010). *Identity texts: The collaborative creation of power in multilingual schools*. Oakhill: Trentham Books.

Das, A. K. L., & Hatlebakk, M. (2010). *Statistical evidence on social and economic exclusion in Nepal*. Kathmandu: Himal Books.

Davis, K. A. (1990). Language policy, class, and schooling in multilingual contexts: The case of Luxembourg. *Language, Culture, and Curriculum*, *3*(2), 125–140.

Davis, K. A. (1991). Socioeconomic transitions and language status change: The case of Luxembourg. In U. Ammon & M. Hellinger (Eds.), *Status change of languages* (pp. 140–163). Berlin: de Gruyter.

Davis, K. A. (1994). *Language planning in multilingual contexts: Policies, communities, and schools in Luxembourg*. Amsterdam/Philadelphia: John Benjamins.

Davis, K. A. (1999). The sociopolitical dynamics of indigenous language maintenance and loss: A framework for language policy and planning. In T. Huebner & K. A. Davis (Eds.), *Sociopolitical perspectives on language policy and planning in the USA* (pp. 67–97). Amsterdam: John Benjamins.

Davis, K. A. (2009). Agentive youth research: Towards individual, collective, and policy transformations. In T. G. Wiley, J. S. Lee, & R. Rumberger (Eds.), *The education of language minority immigrants in the United States* (pp. 202–239). Clevedon: Multilingual Matters.

Davis, K. A. (2014). Engaged language policy and practices. *Language Policy*, *13*(2), 83–100.

Davis, K. A., & Phyak, P. (2015). In the face of neoliberal adversity: Engaging language education policy and practices. *L2 Journal*, 7(3), 146–166.

Davis, K. A., Phyak, P., & Bui, T. T. N. (2012). Multicultural education as community engagement: Policies and planning in a transnational era. *International Journal of Multicultural Education*, *14*(3), 1–19.

Davis, K. A., Cho, H., Ishida, M., Soria, J., & Bazzi, S. (2005). "It's our *Kuleana*": A critical participatory approach to language minority education. In L. Pease-Alvarez & S. R. Schecter (Eds.), *Learning, teaching, and community* (pp. 3–25). Mahwah, NJ: Lawrence Erlbaum Associates.

Delgado, R. (1989). Storytelling for oppositionists and others: A plea for narrative. *Michigan Law Review*, 87, 2411–2441.

Denzin, N. K., & Lincoln, Y. S. (Eds.) (2005). *The handbook of qualitative research* (3rd ed.). Thousand Oaks, CA: Sage.

Deutsch, M. (1974). Awakening the sense of injustice. In M. Lerner & M. Ross (Eds.), *The quest for justice: Myth, reality, ideal* (pp. 1–43). Montreal: Holt, Rinehart & Winston.

Dick, G. S., & McCarty, T. L. (1992). Navajo language maintenance and development: Possibilities for community-controlled schools. *Journal of Navajo Education*, *11*(3), 11–16.

Dorian, N. (1994). Purism vs. compromise in language revitalization and language revival. *Language in Society*, *23*(4), 479–494.

Dorian, N. (1998). Western language ideologies and small-language prospects. In L. A. Grenoble & L. J. Whaley (Eds.), *Endangered languages: Language loss and community response* (pp. 3–21). Cambridge: Cambridge University Press.

Duff, P. (2004). Intertextuality and hybrid discourses: The infusion of pop culture in educational discourse. *Linguistics and Education*, *14*(3–4), 231–276.

References

Duncan-Andrade, J., & Morrell, E. (2008). *The art of critical pedagogy: The promise of moving from theory to practice in urban schools.* New York: Peter Lang.

Eckert, P. (2004). Variation and a sense of place. In C. Fought (Ed.), *Sociolinguistic variation: Critical reflections* (pp. 107–118). Oxford: Oxford University Press.

Espinoza-Herrold, M. (2007). Stepping beyond sí se peude: Dichos as a cultural resource in mother-daughter interaction in a Latino family. *Anthropology and Education Quarterly, 38*(3), 260–277.

FactCheck.Org (2015). Facts about the Syrian refugees. Retrieved from www.factcheck.org/2015/11/facts-about-the-syrian-refugees.

Fairclough, N. (1992). *Discourse and social change.* Cambridge: Polity Press.

Fairclough, N. (1999). Global capitalism and critical awareness of language. *Language Awareness, 8*(2), 71–83.

Fairclough, N. (2006). *Language and globalization.* Abingdon: Routledge.

Faltis, C. (2006). *Teaching English learners in elementary school communities: A joint fostering approach.* New York: Merrill.

Farías, M. (2005). Critical language awareness in foreign language learning. *Literatura y lingüística, 16,* 211–222.

Farr, M., & Song, J. (2011). Language ideologies and policies: Multilingualism and education. *Language and Linguistics Compass, 5*(9), 650–665.

Fine, M. (2006). Bearing witness: Methods for researching oppression and resistance: A textbook for critical research. *Social Justice Research, 19*(1), 83–108.

Fine, M. (2009). Postcards from metro America: Reflections on youth participatory action research for urban justice. *The Urban Review, 41*(1), 1–6.

Fine, M., & Ruglis, J. (2009). Circuits and consequences of dispossession: The racialized realignment of the public sphere for US youth. *Transforming Anthropology, 17*(1), 20–33.

Fine, M., & Torre, M. E. (2006). Intimate details participatory action research in prison. *Action Research, 4*(3), 253–269.

Fine, M., & Weis, L. (2003). *Silenced voices and extraordinary conversations: Re-imagining schools.* New York: Teachers College Press.

Fine, M., Roberts, R. A., & Torre, M. E. (with Bloom, J., Burns, A., Chajet, L., Guishard, M., & Payne, Y. A.). (2004). *Echoes of Brown: Youth documenting and performing the legacy of Brown v. Board of Education.* New York: Teachers College Press.

Fishman, J. A. (1980). Minority language maintenance and the ethnic mother tongue school. *The Modern Language Journal, 64*(2), 167–172.

Fishman, J. A. (Ed.) (1985). *The rise and fall of the ethnic revival: Perspectives on language and ethnicity.* Berlin: Walter de Gruyter.

Fishman, J. A. (1987). *Ideology, society and language: The odyssey of Nathan Birnbaum.* Ann Arbor, MI: Karoma.

Fishman, J. A. (1991). *Reversing language shift: Theoretical and empirical foundations of assistance to threatened languages.* Clevedon: Multilingual Matters.

Fishman, J. A. (1992). Three dilemmas of organized efforts to reverse language shift. In U. Ammon & M. Hellinger (Eds.), *Status change of languages* (pp. 285–293). Berlin: Walter de Gruyter.

Fishman, J. A. (2001). Why is it so hard to save a threatened language. In J. A. Fishman (Ed.), *Can threatened languages be saved?* (pp. 17–22). Clevedon: Multilingual Matters.

Flores, N., & García, O. (2013). Linguistic third spaces in education: Teachers' translanguaging across the bilingual continuum. In D. Little, C. Leung, & P. Van

Avermaet (Eds.), *Managing diversity in education: Languages, policies, pedagogies* (pp. 243–256). Bristol: Multilingual Matters

Flores, N., & Rosa, J. (2015). Undoing appropriateness: Raciolinguistic ideologies and language diversity in education. *Harvard Educational Review*, 85(2), 149–171.

Forman, S. (1993). *Diagnosing America: Anthropology and public engagement*. Ann Arbor, MI: University of Michigan Press.

Foucault, M. (1991). Governmentality. In G. Burchell, C. Gordon, & P. Miller (Eds.), *The Foucault effect: Studies in governmentality* (pp. 87–104). Hemel Hempstead: Harvester Wheatsheaf.

Francis, B., Archer, L., & Mau, A. (2009). Language as capital, or language as identity? Chinese complementary school pupils' perspectives on the purposes and benefits of complementary schools. *British Educational Research Journal*, 35(4), 519–538.

Fraser, N. (1990). Rethinking the public sphere: A contribution to the critique of actually existing democracy. *Social Text*, 25/26, 56–80.

Fraser, N. (2005). *Reframing justice*. Assen: Koninklijke van Gorcum.

Fraser, N. (2008). *Scales of justice: Reimagining political space in a globalizing world*. Cambridge: Polity Press.

Freire, P. (1970). *Pedagogy of the oppressed*. New York: Continuum.

Freire, P. (1992). *Pedagogy of hope*. New York: Continuum.

Freire, P. (1998). *Pedagogy of freedom: Ethics, democracy, and civic courage*. Lanham, MD: Rowman & Littlefield.

Freire, P., & Macedo, D. (2000). *Ideology matters*. Lanham, MD: Rowman & Littlefield.

Friedrich, P. (1989). Language, ideology, and political economy. *American Anthropologist*, 91(2), 295–312.

Gal, S. (1989). Language and political economy. *Annual Review of Anthropology*, 18, 345–367.

Gal, S. (2005). Language ideologies compared: Metaphors and circulations of public and private. *Journal of Linguistic Anthropology*, 15(1), 23–37.

Gal, S. (2006). Contradictions of standard language in Europe: Implications for the study of practices and publics. *Social Anthropology*, 14(2), 163–181.

Gandin, L. A. (2006). Creating real alternatives to neo-liberal policies in education: The citizen school project. In M. W. Apple & K. Buras (Eds.), *The subaltern speak: Curriculum, power, and educational struggles* (pp. 217–242). New York: Routledge.

Gandin, L. A., & Apple, M. W. (2002). Challenging neo-liberalism, building democracy: Creating the citizen school in Porto Alegre, Brazil. *Journal of Education Policy*, 17(2), 259–279.

García, O. (2008). Multicultural language awareness and teacher education. In N. Hornberger (Ed.), *Encyclopedia of language and education* (vol. 6, pp. 385–400). New York: Springer.

García, O. (2009). *Bilingual education in the 21st century: A global perspective*. Malden, MA: Wiley-Blackwell.

García, O. (2012). Bilingual community education: Beyond heritage language education and bilingual education in New York. In O. García, Z. Zakharia, & B. Otcu (Eds.), *Bilingual community education and multilingualism: Beyond heritage languages in a global city* (pp. 3–42). Bristol: Multilingual Matters.

García, O. (2013). From diglossia to transglossia: Bilingual and multilingual classrooms in the 21st century. In C. Abello-Contesse, P. M. Chandler, M. D. Lopez-Jimenez, &

R. Chacon-Beltran (Eds.), *Bilingual and multilingual education in the 21st century: Building on experience* (pp. 155–175). Bristol: Multilingual Matters.

García, O., & Flores, N. (2014). Multilingualism and common core state standards in the United States. In S. May (Ed.), *The multilingual turn: Implications for SLA, TESOL, and bilingual education* (pp. 147–166). New York: Routledge.

García, O., & Kleifgen, J. A. (2010). *Educating emergent bilinguals: Policies, programs, and practices for English language learners*. New York: Teachers College Press.

García, O., & Leiva, C. (2014). Theorizing and enacting translanguaging for social justice. In A. Blackledge & A. Creese (Eds.), *Heteroglossia as pedagogy and practice* (pp. 199–216). London: Springer.

Garcia, O., & Li, W. (2014). *Translanguaging: Language, bilingualism and education*. New York: Palgrave Macmillan.

García, O., & Sylvan, C. E. (2011). Pedagogies and practices in multilingual classrooms: Singularities in pluralities. *The Modern Language Journal, 95*(3), 385–400.

García, O., Skutnabb-Kangas, T., & Torres-Guzmán, M. E. (Eds.) (2006). *Imagining multilingual schools: Languages in education and glocalization*. Clevedon: Multilingual Matters.

García, O., Zakharia, Z., & Otcu, B. (2013). *Bilingual community education for American children: Beyond heritage languages in a global city*. Bristol: Multilingual Matters.

Gee, J. P. (2000). The new literacy studies: From 'socially situated' to the work of the social. In D. Barton, M. Hamilton, & R. Ivanič (Eds.), *Situated literacies: Reading and writing in context* (pp. 180–196). New York: Routledge.

Geertz, C. (1983). *Local knowledge: Further essays in interpretive anthropology*. New York: Basic Books.

Gegeo, D. W., & Watson-Gegeo, K. A. (2001). How we know: Kwara'ae rural villagers doing indigenous epistemology. *The Contemporary Pacific, 13*(1), 55–88.

Gegeo, D. W., & Watson-Gegeo, K. A. (2002). Whose knowledge? Epistemological collisions in Solomon Islands community development. *The Contemporary Pacific, 14*(2), 377–409.

Gegeo, D. W., & Watson-Gegeo, K. A. (2013). The critical villager revisited: Continuing transformations of language and education in Solomon Islands. In J. W. Tollefson (Ed.), *Language policy in education: Critical issues* (2nd ed.) (pp. 233–251). Abingdon: Routledge.

Giampapa, F., & Lamoureux, S. A. (2011). Voices from the field: Identity, language, and power in multilingual research settings. *Journal of Language, Identity, and Education, 10*(3), 127–131.

Giri, R. A. (2010). Cultural anarchism: The consequences of privileging languages in Nepal. *Journal of Multilingual and Multicultural Development, 31*(1), 87–100.

Giri, R. A. (2011). Languages and language politics: How invisible language politics produces visible results in Nepal. *Language Problems and Language Planning, 35*(3), 197–221.

Giroux, H. A. (1997). *Pedagogy and the politics of hope: Theory, culture, and schooling*. Boulder, CO: Westview Press.

Gogolin, I. (1997). The monolingual habitus as the common feature in teaching in the language of the majority in different countries. *Per Linguam, 13*(2), 38–49.

González, N., Moll, L., & Amanti, C. (Eds.) (2005). *Funds of knowledge. Theorizing practices in households, communities, and classrooms*. Mahwah, NJ: Lawrence Erlbaum Associates.

Gramsci, A. (1971). *Selections from the prison notebooks*. New York: International.

Grbich, C. (2004). *New approaches in social research*. London: Sage.
Green, J. P. (2002). *High school graduation rates in the United States*. Revised paper prepared for the Black Alliance of Education Options. New York: Manhattan Institute for Policy Research.
Guishard, M. (2009). The false paths, the endless labors, the turns now this way and now that: Participatory action research, mutual vulnerability, and the politics of inquiry. *The Urban Review*, *41*(1), 85–105.
Gupta, A. F. (1997). When mother-tongue education is not preferred. *Journal of Multilingual and Multicultural Development*, *18*(6), 496–506.
Gurung, H. (2006). *From exclusion to inclusion: Socio-political agenda for Nepal*. Lalitpur: Social Inclusion Research Fund, SNV, Nepal.
Gutiérrez, K., Baquedano-López, P., & Álvarez, H. (2001). Literacy as hybridity: Moving beyond bilingualism in urban classrooms. In M. de la Luz Reyes & J. Halcón (Eds.), *The best for our children: Critical perspectives on literacy for Latino students* (pp. 122–141). New York: Teachers College Press.
Habermas, J. (1981). New social movements. *Telos*, *49*, 33–37.
Habermas, J. (1985). *The theory of communicative action* (vol. 2). Boston, MA: Beacon Press.
Habermas, J. (1989). *The structural transformation of the public sphere: An inquiry into a category of bourgeois society*. Cambridge, MA: MIT Press.
Habermas, J. (1996). *Between facts and norms* (trans. William Rehg). Cambridge, MA: MIT Press.
Hachchethu, K. (2003). Democracy and nationalism: Interface between state and ethnicity in Nepal. *Contributions to Nepalese Studies*, *30*(2), 217–252.
Hajek, J., & Slaughter, Y. (Eds.) (2015). *Challenging the monolingual mindset: Reconsidering Australia's language potential*. Clevedon: Multilingual Matters.
Hall, S. (1996). The problem of ideology: Marxism without guarantees. In D. Morley & K.-H. Chen (Eds.), *Stuart Hall: Critical dialogues in cultural studies* (pp. 24–45). London: Routledge.
Hangen, S. I. (2010). *The rise of ethnic politics in Nepal: Democracy in the margins*. New York: Routledge.
Harvey, D. (2004). *A geographer's perspective on the new American imperialism: Conversations with history*. Berkeley, CA: UC Institute of International Studies.
Harvey, D. (2005). *A brief history of neoliberalism*. Oxford: Oxford University Press.
Harvey, J. (1999). *Civilized oppression*. Lanham, MD: Rowman & Littlefield.
Hawkins, E. (1984). *Awareness of language: An introduction*. Cambridge: Cambridge University Press.
Heath, S. B. (1983). *Ways with words: Language, life, and work in communities and classrooms*. Cambridge: Cambridge University Press.
Heller, M. (2010). The commodification of language. *Annual Review of Anthropology*, *39*, 101–114.
Hélot, C. (2007). *Du bilinguisme en famille au plurilinguisme à l'école*. Paris: L'Harmattan.
Hélot, C. (2011). Children's literature in the multilingual classroom: Developing multilingual literacy acquisition. In C. Hélot & M. O'Laoire (Eds.), *Language policy for the multilingual classroom: Pedagogy of the possible* (pp. 42–64). Bristol: Multilingual Matters.
Hélot, C., & O'Laoire, M. (Eds.) (2011). *Language policy for the multilingual classroom: Pedagogy of the possible*. Bristol: Multilingual Matters.
Hélot, C., & Young, A. S. (2006). Imagining multilingual education in France: A language and cultural awareness project at primary level. In T. Skutnabb-Kangas, O. García,

& M. E. Torres-Guzmán (Eds.), *Imagining multilingual schools* (pp. 69–90). Clevedon: Multilingual Matters.

Holborow, M. (2015). *Language and neoliberalism*. Abingdon: Routledge.

Holt, M., & Gubbins, P (2002). Introduction. In M. Holt & P. Gubbins (Eds.), *Beyond boundaries: Language and identity in contemporary Europe*. Clevedon: Multilingual matters.

hooks, b. (1994). *Teaching to transgress: Education as the practice of freedom*. New York: Routledge.

hooks, b. (2003). *Teaching community: A pedagogy of hope*. New York: Routledge.

Hornberger, N. H. (1988). *Bilingual education and language maintenance: A southern Peruvian Quechua case*. Berlin: Mouton de Gruyter.

Hornberger, N. H. (1989). Can Peru's rural schools be agents for Quechua language maintenance? *Journal of Multilingual & Multicultural Development*, *10*(2), 145–159.

Hornberger, N. H., & Johnson, D. C. (2007). Slicing the onion ethnographically: Layers and spaces in multilingual language education policy and practice. *TESOL Quarterly*, *41*(3), 509–532.

Hornberger, N. H., & Link, H. (2012). Translanguaging and transnational literacies in multilingual classrooms: A biliteracy lens. *International Journal of Bilingual Education and Bilingualism*, *15*(3), 261–278.

Hornberger, N. H., & McCarty, T. L. (2012). Globalization from the bottom up: Indigenous language planning and policy across time, space, and place. *International Multilingual Research Journal*, *6*(1), 1–7.

Hornberger, N. H., & Swinehart, K. F. (2012). Not just situaciones de la vida: Professionalization and Indigenous language revitalization in the Andes. *International Multilingual Research Journal*, *6*(1), 35–49.

Horner, K. (2009). Language policy mechanisms and social practices in multilingual Luxembourg. *Language Problems & Language Planning*, *33*(2), 101–111.

Hough, D., Thapa-Magar, R. B., & Yonjan-Tamang, A. (2009). Privileging indigenous knowledges: Empowering MLE in Nepal. In T. Skutnabb-Kangas, R. Phillipson, A. Mohanty, & M. Panda (Eds.), *Social justice through multilingual education* (pp. 159–176). Bristol: Multilingual Matters.

Hu, G. W. (2005). English language education in China: Policies, progress, and problems. *Language Policy*, *4*(1), 5–24.

Huberman, M. (2001). Networks that alter teaching: Conceptualisations, exchanges and experiments. In J. Soler, A. Craft, & H. Burgess (Eds.), *Teacher development: Exploring our own practice* (pp. 141–159). London: Paul Chapman Publishing.

Huebner, T., & Davis, K. (Eds.) (1999). *Sociopolitical perspectives on language policy and planning in the USA*. Amsterdam: John Benjamins.

Hult, F. M., & Johnson, D. C. (2015). *Research methods in language policy and planning: A practical guide*. Chichester: John Wiley & Sons.

Hymes, D. (ed.) (1969). *Reinventing anthropology*. New York: Vintage Books.

Hymes, D. (1974). *Foundations in sociolinguistics: An ethnographic approach*. Philadelphia, PA: University of Pennsylvania Press.

Hymes, D. (1980). *Language in education: Ethnolinguistic essays*. Washington, DC: Center for Applied Linguistics.

Hymes, D., & Fought, J. (1981). *American structuralism*. The Hague: Mouton.

Hymes, D. H. (1991). *Ethnographic monitoring of children's acquisition of reading/language arts skills in and out of the classroom, vols. 1–3: Final report*. Philadelphia, PA: Graduate School of Education, University of Pennsylvania.

Hymes, D. H. (1996). *Ethnography, linguistics, narrative inequality: Toward an understanding of voice*. London: Taylor & Francis.

Irvine, J. T. (1989). When talk isn't cheap: Language and political economy. *American Ethnologist, 16*(2), 248–267.

Irvine, J. T., & Gal, S. (2000). Language ideology and linguistic differentiation. In P. V. Kroskrity (Ed.), *Regimes of language: Ideologies, polities, and identities* (pp. 35–84). Santa Fe, NM: School of American Research Press.

Jaffe, A. (1999). *Ideologies in action: Language politics on Corsica*. Berlin: Walter de Gruyter.

Jaffe, A. (2009). The production and reproduction of language ideologies in practice. In N. Coupland & A. Jaworski (Eds.), *The new sociolinguistics reader* (pp. 390–404). New York: Palgrave Macmillan.

Johnson, D. C. (2009). Ethnography of language policy. *Language Policy, 8*(2), 139–159.

Johnson, D. C. (2013). *Language policy*. New York: Palgrave Macmillan.

Johnson, D. C., & Ricento, T. (2013). Conceptual and theoretical perspectives in language planning and policy: Situating the ethnography of language policy. *International Journal of the Sociology of Language, 219*, 7–21.

Joseph, M., & Ramani, E. (2012). "Glocalization": Going beyond the dichotomy of global versus local through additive multilingualism. *International Multilingual Research Journal, 6*(1), 22–34.

Kanno, Y. (2003). Imagined communities, school visions, and the education of bilingual students in Japan. *Journal of Language, Identity, and Education, 2*(4), 285–300.

Kemmis, S., & McTaggart, R. (2005). Communicative action and the public sphere. In N. K. Denzin & Y. S. Lincoln (Eds.), *The Sage handbook of qualitative research* (pp. 559–603). Thousand Oaks, CA: Sage.

Kent, N. (2004). *Hawai'i Islands under the influence*. Honolulu, HI: University of Hawai'i Press.

Khubchandani, L. M. (2003). Defining mother tongue education in plurilingual contexts. *Language Policy, 2*(3), 239–254.

King, K. A. (2001). *Language revitalization processes and prospects: Quichua in the Ecuadorian Andes*. Clevedon: Multilingual Matters.

Kirkpatrick, A. (2013). The lingua franca approach to the teaching of English: A possible pathway to genuine multilingualism in local languages and English. In H. McIlwraith (Ed.), *Multilingual education in Africa: Lessons from the Juba language-in-education conference* (pp. 11–16). London: British Council.

Kosonen, K., & Young, C. (Eds.) (2009). *Mother tongue as bridge language of instruction: Policies and experiences in Southeast Asia*. Bangkok: SEAMEO.

Kramsch, C. (Ed.) (2002). *Language acquisition and language socialization*. London: Continuum.

Kramsch, C. (2009). *The multilingual subject*. Oxford: Oxford University Press.

Kroskrity, P. V. (2004). Language ideologies. In A. Duranti (Ed.), *A companion to linguistic anthropology* (pp. 496–517). Malden, MA: Blackwell.

Kroskrity, P. V. (2009). Language renewal as sites of language ideological struggle: The need for ideological clarification. In J. Reyhner & L. Lockard (Eds.), *Indigenous language revitalization: Encouragement, guidance and lessons learned* (pp. 71–83). Flagstaff, AZ: Northern Arizona University.

Labov, W. (1972). *Language in the inner city: Studies in the Black English vernacular.* Philadelphia, PA: University of Pennsylvania Press.

Labov, W. (1982). Objectivity and commitment in linguistic science: The case of the Black English trial in Ann Arbor. *Language in Society, 11*(2), 165–201.

Lam, W. S. E. (2000). L2 literacy and the design of the self: A case study of a teenager writing on the Internet. *TESOL Quarterly, 34*(3), 457–482.

Lambert, B. W., & Cohen, N. E. (1949). A comparison of different types of self-surveys. *Journal of Social Issues, 5*(2), 46–56.

Lather, P. (2004). This is your father's paradigm: Government intrusion and the case of qualitative research in education. *Qualitative Inquiry, 10*(1), 15–34.

Laviña-Gumba, L. (2015). Mother-tongue-based literacy, a tool for indigenous people's empowerment: The Western Subanon and Binukid/Higaonon experience. In H Coleman (Ed.), *Language and social cohesion in the developing world* (pp. 144–154). Colombo: British Council and Deutsche Gesellschaft für Internationale Zusammenarbeit.

Lawoti, M. (2010). Informal institutions and exclusion in democratic Nepal. *Himalaya, 28*(1). Retrieved from http://digitalcommons.macalester.edu/himalaya/vol28/iss1/2.

Lee, T. S. (2009). Language, identity, and power: Navajo and pueblo young adults' perspectives and experiences with competing language ideologies. *Journal of Language, Identity, and Education, 8*(5), 307–320.

Lee, T. S. (2014). Critical language awareness among native youth in New Mexico. In L. T. Wyman, T. L. McCarty, & S. E. Nicholas (Eds.), *Indigenous youth and multilingualism: Language identity, ideology, and practice in dynamic cultural worlds* (pp. 130–148). New York: Routledge.

Leeman, J., Rabin, L., & Román-Mendoza, E. (2011). Identity and activism in heritage language education. *Modern Language Journal, 95*(4), 481–495.

Lefebvre, H. (1991). *The production of space*. Oxford: Blackwell.

Lefebvre, H. (1996). *Writings on cities*. Cambridge, MA: Blackwell.

Lewis, G., Jones, B., & Baker, C. (2012). Translanguaging: Developing its conceptualisation and contextualisation. *Educational Research and Evaluation, 18*(7), 655–670.

Li, W. (2011a). Moment analysis and translanguaging space: Discursive construction of identities by multilingual Chinese youth in Britain. *Journal of Pragmatics, 43*(5), 1222–1235.

Li, W. (2011b). Multilinguality, multimodality, and multicompetence: Code- and modeswitching by minority ethnic children in complementary schools. *The Modern Language Journal, 95*(3), 370–384.

Li, W. (2014). Who's teaching whom? Co-learning in multilingual classrooms. In S. May (Ed.), *The multilingual turn: Implications for SLA, TESOL and bilingual education* (pp. 176–190). New York: Routledge.

Li, W., & Zhu, H. (2013). Translanguaging identities and ideologies: Creating transnational space through dynamic multilingual practices amongst Chinese university students in the UK. *Applied Linguistics, 34*(5), 516–535.

Lin, A. M. Y. (2013). Breaking the hegemonic knowledge claim in language policy and education: The global south as method. In J. A. Shoba & F. Chimbutane (Eds.),

Bilingual education and language policy in the global south (pp. 223–231). New York: Routledge.

Lin, A. M. Y. (2014). Critical discourse analysis in applied linguistics: A methodological review. *Annual Review of Applied Linguistics, 34*, 213–232.

Lin, A. M. Y., & Martin, P. (Eds.) (2005). *Decolonization, globalization: Language-in-education policy and practice*. Clevedon: Multilingual Matters.

Lin, A. M. Y., Wang, W., Akamatsu, A., & Riazi, M. (2002). Appropriating English, expanding identities, and re-visioning the field: From TESOL to teaching English for glocalized communication (TEGCOM). *Journal of Language, Identity, and Education, 1*(4), 295–316.

Lipman, P. (2011). *The new political economy of urban education: Neoliberalism, race, and the right to the city*. Abingdon: Routledge.

Lippi-Green, R. (1997). *English with an accent: Language, ideology, and discrimination in the United States*. Abingdon: Routledge.

Lippi-Green, R. (2000). That's not my language: The struggle to (re)define African American English. In R. D. González & I. Melis (Eds.), *Language ideologies: Critical perspectives on the official English movement: Education and the social implications of official language* (pp. 230–247). Mahwah, NJ: Lawrence Erlbaum Associates.

Lo Bianco, J. (1999). The language of policy: What sort of policy-making is the officialization of English in the United States? In T. Huebner & K. A. Davis (Eds.), *Sociopolitical perspectives on language policy and planning in the USA* (pp. 39–66). Amsterdam: Benjamins.

López, L. E. (2006). Cultural diversity, multilingualism and indigenous education in Latin America. In T. Skutnabb-Kangas, O. García, & M. Torres-Guzmán (Eds.), *Imagining multilingual schools* (pp. 238–261). Clevedon: Multilingual Matters.

Low, S. M., & Merry, S. E. (2010). Engaged anthropology: Diversity and dilemmas. *Current Anthropology, 51*(2), 203–226.

Luke, A. (1996). Series editor's introduction. In D. Hymes, *Ethnography, linguistics, narrative inequality: Toward an understanding of voice* (pp. vii–ix). London: Taylor & Francis.

Luke, A. (2002). Beyond science and ideology critique: Developments in critical discourse analysis. *Annual Review of Applied Linguistics, 22*, 96–110.

Luke, A. (2011). Generalizing across borders: Policy and the limits of education science. *Educational Researcher, 40*(8), 367–377.

Luke, A., Luke, C., & Graham, P. (2007). Globalization, corporatism, and critical language education. *International Multilingual Research Journal, 1*(1), 1–13.

Macedo, D. (2000). Introduction. In P. Freire, *Pedagogy of the oppressed* (pp. 11–28). New York: Bloomsbury Publishing.

Madison, D. S. (2012). *Critical ethnography: Method, ethics, and performance*. Thousand Oaks, CA: Sage.

Makalela, L. (2014). Teaching indigenous African languages to speakers of other African languages: The effects of translanguaging for multilingual development. In L. Hibbert & C. van der Walt (Eds.), *Multilingual universities in South Africa: Reflecting society in higher education* (pp. 88–104). Bristol: Multilingual Matters.

Makihara, M., & Schieffelin, B. B. (Eds.) (2007). *Consequences of contact: Language ideologies and sociocultural transformations in Pacific societies*. Oxford: Oxford University Press.

Makoni, S., & Pennycook, A. (2005). Disinventing and (re)constituting languages. *Critical Inquiry in Language Studies: An International Journal, 2*(3), 137–156.

Makoni, S., & Pennycook, A. (Eds.) (2007). *Disinventing and reconstituting languages*. Clevedon: Multilingual Matters.

Mallett, K. E., Bigelow, M., Krashen, S., Matsuda, P., & Reyes, S. (2010). Linking academic and advocacy interests among AAAL members. Special session presented at the annual meeting of the American Association for Applied Linguistics (AAAL), Atlanta, GA.

Malsbary, C. B., & Appelgate, M. H. (2016). Working downstream: A beginning EL teacher negotiating policy and practice. *Language Policy*, 15(1), 27–47.

Manan, S. A., David, M. K., & Dumanig, F. P. (2016). Language management: A snapshot of governmentality within the private schools in Quetta, Pakistan. *Language Policy*, 15(1), 3–26.

Marcus, G. E. (1994). What comes (just) after "post"? The case of ethnography. In N. K. Denzin & Y. S. Lincoln (Eds.), *Handbook of qualitative research* (pp. 563–574). Thousand Oaks, CA: Sage.

Marcus, G. E., & Fischer, M. M. J. (1986). *Anthropology as cultural critique*. Chicago, IL: University of Chicago Press.

Martin, P., Bhatt, A., Bhojani, N., & Creese, A. (2006). Managing bilingual interaction in a Gujarati complementary school in Leicester. *Language and Education*, 20(1), 5–22.

Martin-Baró, I. (1994). *Writings for a liberation psychology* (trans. A. Aron and S. Corne). Cambridge, MA: Harvard University Press.

Martinez-Alier, J. (2002). *The environmentalism of the poor: A study of ecological conflicts and valuation*. Cheltenham: Edward Elgar Publishing.

Martin-Jones, M., Blackledge, A., & Creese, A. (Eds.) (2012). *The Routledge handbook of multilingualism*. Abingdon: Routledge.

Mathers, A., & Novelli, M. (2007). Researching resistance to neoliberal globalization: Engaged ethnography as solidarity and praxis. *Globalizations*, 4(2), 229–249.

May, S. (2008). Bilingual/immersion education: What the research tells us. In J. Cummins & N. H. Hornberger (Eds.), *Encyclopedia of language and education (2nd ed., vol. 5): Bilingual education* (pp. 19–33). New York: Springer.

May, S. (2012). *Language and minority rights: Ethnicity, nationalism and the politics of language* (2nd ed.). New York: Routledge.

May, S. (Ed.) (2014). *The multilingual turn: Implications for SLA, TESOL, and bilingual education*. Abingdon: Routledge.

McCarty, T. L. (2002). *A place to be Navajo: Rough Rock and the struggle for self-determination in Indigenous schooling*. Mahwah, NJ: Lawrence Erlbaum Associates.

McCarty, T. L. (2003). Revitalising indigenous languages in homogenising times. *Comparative education*, 39(2), 147–163.

McCarty, T. L. (Ed.) (2011). *Ethnography and language policy*. New York: Routledge.

McCarty, T. L. (2014). Negotiating sociolinguistic borderlands: Native youth language practices in space, time, and place. *Journal of Language, Identity, and Education*, 13(4), 254–267.

McCarty, T. L., & Schaffer, R. (1992). Language and literacy. In J. Reyhner (Ed.), *Teaching American Indian students* (pp. 115–131). Norman, OK: University of Oklahoma Press.

McCarty, T. L., & Warhol, L. (2011). The anthropology of language policy and planning. In B. A. Levinson & M. Pollock (Eds.), *A companion to the anthropology of education* (pp. 177–196). Oxford: Wiley-Blackwell.

McCarty, T. L., & Wyman, L. T. (2009). Indigenous youth and bilingualism: Theory, research, praxis. *Journal of Language, Identity, and Education*, 8(5), 279–290.

McCarty, T. L., Collins, J., & Hopson, R. K. (2011). Dell Hymes and the new language policy studies: Update from an underdeveloped country. *Anthropology & Education Quarterly*, *42*(4), 335–363.

McCarty, T. L., Zepeda, O., & Romero, M. E. (2006). Reclaiming the gift: Indigenous youth counter-narratives on native language loss and revitalization. *The American Indian Quarterly*, *30*(1), 28–48.

McGroarty, M. (2006). Neoliberal collusion or strategic simultaneity? On multiple rationales for language-in-education policies. *Language Policy*, *5*(1), 3–13.

McGroarty, M. (2013). Multiple actors and arenas in evolving language policy. In J. W. Tollefson (Ed.), *Language policies in education: Critical issues* (2nd ed.) (pp. 35–57). Abingdon: Routledge.

McNally, D. (2011). *Monsters of the market: Zombies, vampires, and global capitalism*. Boston, MA: Brill.

Menken, K. (2013). Restrictive language education policies and emergent bilingual youth: A perfect storm with imperfect outcomes. *Theory into Practice*, *52*(3), 160–168.

Menken, K., & García, O. (Eds.) (2010). *Negotiating language policies in schools: Educators as policymakers*. New York: Routledge.

Milroy, J. (2001). Language ideologies and the consequences of standardization. *Journal of Sociolinguistics*, *5*(4), 530–555.

Ministry of Education. (2010). *Manual for implementing multilingual education*. Bhaktapur: Department of Education.

Mohanty, A. K. (2006). Multilingualism of the unequals and predicaments of education in India: Mother tongue or other tongue. In O. García, T. Skutnabb-Kangas, & M. E. Torres-Guzmán (Eds.), *Imagining multilingual schools: Languages in education and glocalization* (pp. 262–279). Clevedon: Multilingual Matters.

Mohanty, A. K., Mishra, M. K., Reddy, N. U., & Ramesh, G. (2009). Overcoming the language barrier for tribal children: MLE in Andhra Pradesh and Orissa, India. In A. Mohanty, M. Panda, R. Phillipson, & T. Skutnabb-Kangas (Eds.), *Multilingual education for social justice: Globalising the local* (pp. 278–291). New Delhi: Orient BlackSwan.

Moll, L., Amanti, C., Neff, D., & González, N. (1992). Funds of knowledge for teaching: Using a qualitative approach to connect homes and classrooms. *Theory into Practice*, *31*(2), 132–141.

Montecinos, C. (1995). Culture as an ongoing dialogue: Implications for multicultural teacher education. In C. Sleeter & P. McLaren (Eds.), *Multicultural education, critical pedagogy, and the politics of difference* (pp. 269–308). Albany, NY: State University of New York Press.

Moore, H. (1996). Language policies as virtual reality: Two Australian examples. *TESOL Quarterly*, *30*(3), 473–497.

Morrell, E. (2008). *Critical literacy and urban youth: Pedagogies of access, dissent, and liberation*. New York: Routledge.

Norton, B. (2000). *Identity and language learning*. London: Longman.

Ochs, E., & Schieffelin, B. (2009). Language acquisition and socialization: Three developmental stories and their implications. In A. Duranti (Ed.), *Linguistic anthropology: A reader* (pp. 296–328). Malden, MA: Wiley-Blackwell.

Orfield, G., Losen, D., Wald, J., & Swanson, C. B. (2004). *Losing our future: How minority youth are being left behind by the graduation rate crisis*. Cambridge, MA: Harvard Education Publishing Group.

Orman, J. (2008). *Language policy and nation-building in post-apartheid South Africa*. Heidelberg: Springer.

Otheguy, R., García, O., & Reid, W. (2015). Clarifying translanguaging and deconstructing named languages: A perspective from linguistics. *Applied Linguistics Review*, 6(3), 281–307.

Pan, L. (2011). English language ideologies in the Chinese foreign language education policies: A world-system perspective. *Language Policy*, 10(3), 245–263.

Pandey, D. R. (2012). The legacy of Nepal's failed development. In S. von Einsiedel, D. M. Malone, & S. Pradhan (Eds.), *Nepal in transition: From people's war to fragile peace* (pp. 81–99). Cambridge: Cambridge University Press.

Park, J. S. Y., & Wee, L. (2012). *Markets of English: Linguistic capital and language policy in a globalizing world*. Abingdon: Routledge.

Patiño Santos, A. (2011). Negotiating power relations and ethnicity in a sociolinguistic ethnography in Madrid. *Journal of Language, Identity, and Education*, 10(3), 145–163.

Pavlenko, A., & Blackledge, A. (Eds.) (2004). *Negotiation of identities in multilingual contexts*. Bristol: Multilingual Matters.

PBS (2013). *Syrian refugees*. Retrieved from www.pbs.org/newshour/multimedia/refugees-syria.

Pennycook, A. D. (1994). *The cultural politics of English as in international language*. London: Longman.

Pennycook, A. D. (2007). Language, localization, and the real: Hip-hop and the global spread of authenticity. *Journal of Language, Identity, and Education*, 6(2), 101–115.

Pennycook, A. D. (2010). *Language as a local practice*. Abingdon: Routledge.

Pennycook, A. D. (2013). Language policies, language ideologies and local language practices. In L. Wee, R. B. Goh, & L. Lim (Eds.), *The politics of English: South Asia, Southeast Asia and the Asia Pacific* (pp. 1–18). Amsterdam: John Benjamins.

Philips, S. (1983). *The invisible culture: Communication in classroom and community on the Warm Springs Indian Reservation*. New York: Longman.

Phillipson, R. (1988). Linguicism: Structures and ideologies in linguistic imperialism. In J. Cummins & T. Skuttnab-Kangas (Eds.), *Minority education: From shame to struggle* (pp. 339–358). Clevedon: Multilingual Matters.

Phillipson, R. (1992). *Linguistic imperialism*. Oxford: Oxford University Press.

Phillipson, R. (2008). The linguistic imperialism of neoliberal empire. *Critical Inquiry in Language Studies*, 5(1), 1–43.

Phillipson, R. (2012). Linguistic imperialism alive and kicking. *The Guardian*, March 13. Retrieved from www.guardian.co.uk/education/2012/mar/13/linguistic-imperialism-english-language-teaching.

Phyak, P. (2011). Beyond the façade of language planning for Nepalese primary education: Monolingual hangover, elitism and displacement of local languages? *Current Issues in Language Planning*, 12(2), 265–287.

Phyak, P. (2013). Language ideologies and local languages as the medium-of-instruction policy: A critical ethnography of a multilingual school in Nepal. *Current Issues in Language Planning*, 14(1), 127–143.

Phyak, P. (2016a). Local-global tension in the ideological construction of English language education policy in Nepal. In R. Kirkpatrick (Ed.), *English language education policy in Asia* (pp. 199–217). New York: Springer.

Phyak, P. (2016b). For our cho:tlung': Decolonizing language ideologies and (re) imagining multilingual education policies and practices in Nepal. (Unpublished doctoral dissertation). University of Hawai'i.

Phyak, P., & Bui, T. (2014). Youth engaging language policy: Ideologies and transformations from within. *Language Policy*, *13*(2), 101–120.

Pickford, S. (2005). Emerging pedagogies of linguistic and cultural continuity in Papua New Guinea. *Language, Culture and Curriculum*, *18*(2), 139–153.

Pietikäinen, S., & Kelly-Holmes, H. (Eds.) (2013). *Multilingualism and the periphery*. Oxford: Oxford University Press.

Piller, I. (2016). *Linguistic diversity and social justice: An introduction to applied sociolinguistics*. Oxford: Oxford University Press.

Piller, I., & Cho, J. (2013). Neoliberalism as language policy. *Language in Society*, *42*(1), 23–44.

Portante, D., & Max, C. (2008). Plurilingualism and multilingual literacy among young learners in Luxembourg. In C. Kenner & T. Hickey (Eds.), *Multilingual Europe: Diversity and learning* (pp. 124–130). Oakhill: Trentham Books.

Porto Alegre City Secretariat of Education (1999). Cycles of formation: Political-pedagogical proposal for the citizen's school. *Cadernos Pedagogicos*, *9*(1), 1–111.

Poudyal, C. S. (2013). Private schooling and Fayol's principles of management: A case from Nepal. *Journal of Education and Research*, *3*(1), 6–23.

Poythress, K. (2010, September 11). The impact of private schools on public education. *Civil Beat*. Retrieved from www.civilbeat.com/2010/09/4031-the-impact-of-private-schools-on-public-education.

Purcell, M. (2002). Excavating Lefebvre: The right to the city and its urban politics of the inhabitant. *GeoJournal*, *58*(2–3), 99–108.

Purcell, M. (2009). Resisting neoliberalization: Communicative planning or counter-hegemonic movements? *Planning Theory*, *8*(2), 140–165.

Rai, V.S, Rai, M., Phyak, P., & Rai, N. (2011). *Multilingual education in Nepal: Hearsay and reality*. Kathmandu: UNESCO.

Ramanathan, V. (2005). Rethinking language planning and policy from the ground up: Refashioning institutional realities and human lives. *Current Issues in Language Planning*, *6*(2), 89–101.

Ramanathan, V. (2006). Gandhi, non-cooperation, and socio-civic education in Gujarat, India: Harnessing the vernaculars. *Journal of Language, Identity, and Education*, *5*(3), 229–250.

Ramanathan, V. (Ed.) (2013). *Language policies and (dis)citizenship: Rights, access, pedagogies*. Buffalo, NY: Multilingual Matters.

Ramani, E., & Joseph, M. (2010). *Developing academic biliteracy: A case study of a bilingual BA degree (in English and Sesotho sa Leboa)*. The University of Limpopo (unpublished manuscript).

Rampton, B. (1995). *Crossings: Language and ethnicity among adolescents*. London: Longman.

Regmi, K. D. (2016). World Bank in Nepal's education: Three decades of neoliberal reform. *Globalisation, Societies and Education*, doi:10.1080/14767724.2016.1169517.

Ricento, T. (2006). Language policy: Theory and practice: An introduction. In T. Ricento (Ed.), *An introduction to language policy: Theory and method* (pp. 10–23). Malden, MA: Blackwell.

Ricento, T. (Ed.) (2015). *Language policy and political economy: English in a global context*. New York: Oxford University Press.

Rockwell, R. E., Andre, L. C., & Hawley, M. K. (2010). *Families and educators as partners*. Belmont, CA: Wadsworth/Cengage Learning.

Ruiz, R. (1984). Orientations in language planning. *NABE Journal, 8*(2), 346–361.

Schensul, J. J., & Schensul, S. L. (1992). Collaborative research: Methods of inquiry for social change. In M. D. LeCompte, W. L. Millroy, & J. Preissle (Eds.), *Handbook of qualitative research in education* (pp. 161–200). San Diego, CA: Academic Press.

Shakya, S. (2009). *Unleashing Nepal: Past, present and the future of the economy*. New Delhi: Penguin Books.

Shohamy, E. (2006). *Language policy: Hidden agendas and new approaches*. New York: Routledge.

Silverstein, M. (1979). Language structure and linguistic ideology. In P. R. Clyne, W. F. Hanks, & C. L. Hofbauer (Eds.), *The elements: A parasession on linguistic units and levels* (pp. 193–247). Chicago, IL: Chicago Linguistic Society.

Skutnabb-Kangas, T. (1990). Legitimating or delegitimating new forms of racism: The role of the researcher. *Journal of Multilingual Development, 11*(1–2), 77–99.

Skutnabb-Kangas, T., & Heugh, K. (Eds.) (2012). *Multilingual education and sustainable diversity work: From periphery to center*. New York: Routledge.

Skutnabb-Kangas, T., Phillipson, R., Mohanty, A. K., & Panda, M. (Eds.) (2009). *Social justice through multilingual education*. Toronto: Multilingual Matters.

Smith, L. T. (1999). *Decolonizing methodologies: Research and indigenous peoples*. New York: Zed Books.

Smith, L. T. (2005). On tricky ground: Researching the native in the age of uncertainty. In N. K. Denzin & Y. S. Lincoln (Eds.), *Handbook of qualitative research* (3rd ed.). Thousand Oaks, CA: Sage.

Smith, L. T. (2012). *Decolonizing methodologies: Research and indigenous peoples* (2nd ed.). London: Zed Books.

Smith, N. (2003). *American empire. Roosevelt's geographer and the prelude to globalization*. Berkeley, CA: University of California Press.

Souto-Manning, M., & Swick, K. J. (2006). Teachers' beliefs about parents and family involvement: Rethinking our family involvement paradigm. *Early Childhood Education Journal, 34*(2), 187–193.

Steger, M., Goodman, J., & Wilson, E. K. (2012). *Justice globalism: Ideology, crises, policy*. London: Sage.

Stoudt, B. G., Fox, M., & Fine, M. (2011). Awakening injustice in a new century. In P. T. Coleman (Ed.), *Conflict, interdependence, and injustice* (pp. 165–191). New York: Springer.

Street, B. V. (1995). *Social literacies: Critical approaches to literacy in development, ethnography and education*. London: Longman.

Street, B. V. (2000). Literacy events and literacy practices. In M. Martin-Jones & K. Jones (Eds.), *Multilingual Literacies: Comparative Perspectives on Research and Practice* (pp. 17–29). Amsterdam: John Benjamins.

Susser, I. (2010). The anthropologist as social critic: Working toward a more engaged anthropology. *Current Anthropology, 51*(2), 227–233.

Talmy, S. (2004). Forever FOB: The cultural production of ESL in a high school. *Pragmatics, 14*(2/3), 149–172.

Taylor-Leech, K. (2013). Finding space for non-dominant languages in education: Language policy and medium of instruction in Timor-Leste 2000–2012. *Current Issues in Language Planning, 14*(1), 109–126.

Tenery, M. F. (2005). La visita. In N. González, L. C. Moll, & C. Amanti (Eds.), *Funds of knowledge: Theorizing in households, communities and classrooms* (pp. 119–139). Abingdon: Routledge.

Thomas, W. P., & Collier, V. P. (2000). Accelerated schooling for all students: Research findings on education in multilingual communities. In S. Shaw (Ed.), *Intercultural education in European classrooms* (pp. 15–35). Stoke-on-Trent: Trentham Books.

Thomas, W. P., & Collier, V. P. (2002). *A national study of school effectiveness for language minority students' long-term academic achievement*. Santa Cruz, CA: Center for Research on Education, Diversity, and Excellence, University of California at Santa Cruz.

Tollefson, J. W. (1991). *Planning language, planning inequality: Language policy in the community*. London: Longman.

Tollefson, J. W. (Ed.) (1995). *Power and inequality in language education*. Cambridge: Cambridge University Press.

Tollefson, J. W. (2006). Critical theory in language policy. In T. Ricento (Ed.), *An introduction to language policy: Theory and method* (pp. 42–59). Malden, MA: Blackwell.

Tollefson, J. W. (Ed.) (2013). *Language policies in education: Critical issues* (2nd ed.). New York: Routledge.

Torre, M. E. (2005). The alchemy of integrated spaces. In L. Weis & M. Fine (Eds.), *Beyond silenced voices: Class, race, and gender in United States schools* (pp. 251–266). New York: State University of New York Press.

Torre, M. E., & Fine, M. (2004). Re-membering exclusions: Participatory action research in public institutions. *Qualitative Research in Psychology*, 1(1), 15–37.

Torre, M. E., & Fine, M. (2011). A wrinkle in time: Tracing a legacy of public science through community self surveys and participatory action research. *Journal of Social Issues*, 67(1), 106–121.

Treuer, D. (1995). *Little*. New York: Picador USA.

Tsui, A. B., & Tollefson, J. W. (2007). *Language policy, culture, and identity in Asian contexts*. Mahwah, NJ: Lawrence Erlbaum Associates.

Tupas, R. (2015). Inequalities of multilingualism: Challenges to mother tongue-based multilingual education. *Language and Education*, 29(2), 112–124.

UNDP (2014). *Nepal human development report 2014: Beyond geography; unlocking human potential*. Kathmandu: United Nations Development Program.

US Census Bureau (2000). Profile of selected social characteristics: Demographic Profile of foreign-language speakers. Retrieved from www.census.gov/library/publications/2013/acs/acs–22.html.

US Census Bureau (2010). United States Census 2010. Retrieved from www.census.gov/2010census.

Van der Aa, J., & Blommaert, J. M. E. (2011). Ethnographic monitoring: Hymes' unfinished business in educational research. *Anthropology and Education Quarterly*, 42(4), 319–334.

Vasco Correia, S. (2012) "Ziel mär deng Sproochen!": Une reconnaissance des profils linguistiques des élèves pour une École de la cohésion au Luxembourg. University of Luxembourg, Luxembourg (unpublished manuscript).

Velasco, P., & García, O. (2014). Translanguaging and the writing of bilingual learners. *Bilingual Research Journal*, 37(1), 6–23.

Vertovec, S. (2007). Super-diversity and its implications. *Ethnic and Racial Studies*, 30(6), 1024–1054.

Wallen, M., & Kelly-Holmes, H. (2015). Developing language awareness for teachers of emergent bilingual learners using dialogic inquiry. *International Journal of Bilingual Education and Bilingualism*, doi:10.1080/13670050.2015.1051506

Warner, M. (2002). Publics and counterpublics. *Public Culture, 14*(1), 49–90.

Warren, M. R., & Mapp, K. L. (2011). *A match on dry grass: Community organizing as a catalyst for school reform*. Oxford: Oxford University Press.

Warschauer, M. (1999). *Electronic literacies: Language, culture, and power in online education*. Mahway, NJ: Erlbaum.

Weber, J.-J. (2009). Constructing lusobourgish ethnicities: Implications for language-in-education policy. *Language Problems and Language Planning, 33*(2), 132–152.

Weber, J.-J. (2014). *Flexible multilingual education: Putting children's needs first*. Bristol: Multilingual Matters.

Weber, J.-J., & Horner, K. (2012). *Introducing multilingualism: A social approach*. New York: Routledge.

Weinberg, M. (2013). Revisiting history in language policy: The case of medium of instruction in Nepal. *Working Papers in Educational Linguistics, 28*(1), 61–80.

Wiley, T. G. (1996). Language policy and planning. In S. McKay & N. Hornberger (Eds.), *Sociolinguistics and language teaching* (pp. 103–147). Cambridge: Cambridge University Press.

Wiley, T. G. (1999). Comparative historical perspectives in the analysis of US language polices. In T. Heubner & K. A. Davis (Eds.), *Sociopolitical perspectives on language planning and language policy* (pp. 17–37). Amsterdam: John Benjamins.

Wiley, T. G. (2004). Language planning, language policy, and the English-Only Movement. In E. Finegan & J. Rickford (Eds.), *Language in the USA: Themes for the twenty-first century* (pp. 319–338). Cambridge: Cambridge University Press.

Williams, C. (1994). *Arfarniad o ddulliau dysgu ac addysgu yng nghyd-destun addysg uwchradd ddwyieithog* [Appraisal of methods of learning and teaching in the context of bilingual secondary education]. (Unpublished PhD dissertation), University of Wales, Bangor.

Wormser, M. H., & Selltiz, C. (1951). *How to conduct a community self-survey of civil rights*. New York: Association Press.

Wyman, L. T. (2012). *Youth culture, language endangerment and linguistic survivance*. Bristol: Multilingual Matters.

Wyman, L. T., McCarty, T. L., & Nicholas, S. E. (Eds.) (2014). *Indigenous youth and multilingualism: Language identity, ideology, and practice in dynamic cultural worlds*. New York: Routledge.

Young, A., & Hélot, C. (2008). Parent-teacher partnerships: Co-constructing knowledge about languages and cultures in a French primary school. In C. Kenner & T. Hickey (Eds.), *Multilingual Europe: Diversity and learning* (pp. 89–95). Stoke-on-Trent: Trentham Books.

Young, C. (2002). First language first: Literacy education for the future in a multilingual Philippine society. *International Journal of Bilingual Education and Bilingualism, 5*(4), 221–232.

Zentella, A. C. (1997). *Growing up bilingual*. Malden, MA: Blackwell.

Zentella, A. C. (2005). Premises, promises, and pitfalls of language socialization research in Latino families and communities. In A. C. Zentella (Ed.), *Building on strength: Language and literacy in Latino families and communities* (pp. 13–30). New York: Teachers College Press.

INDEX

Alaimaleata, Elisapeta 75
Andre, L. C. 102
anthropology 40–41
Appadurai, A. 54, 61
Arias, M. B. 101
Asian Development Bank 63

bilingual education 48
bilingualism 57, 76
Bourdieu, Pierre 14
Brown v. Board of Education 35–36
bullying 34–35
Burkett, M. 7

Canagarajah, A. S. 58
children: Hawaiian children 52; language practices of 4; in Luxembourg 76; Puerto Rican children 44
China, emphasis on English language education 25
Citizen School (Brazil) 77–78, 111
civilized oppression, Harvey's concept of 33
commodification, of the English language 24–26
Common Core Standards mandate 6, 53, 74, 76
communities of language 48
community engagement 98–104
Community Organizing and School Reform Project 55–57

community-based research and reform 55–57
community-oriented schooling 77–78
complementary schools, translanguaging in 82–86
conscientização 50
corporations 38; multinational 37–38
Creole English 72–74
critical indigenous pedagogy 99
critical language awareness 95–96
critical reflexivity 48–49
critical/political research approach 40–43
Current Anthropology 40

Der Spiegel newspaper 8
discrimination. *see* social justice
dispossession 37
Distinction: A Social Critique of the Judgment of Taste (Bourdieu 1984) 14

Echoes of Brown (Fine et al. 2004) 35–36
economic globalization. *see* neoliberalism
education, English/Western 61
education advocacy 48
educational inequality, addressing 81–82
engaged ethnography: research 43–49; as sociopolitical practice 49–53
Engaged language policy and practices (ELP) 1-5, 39–49
England 83, 84

English language: commodification of 24–26; discourse on 3; and "quality education" 67
equity issues, ELP approach 10–11
ethnography, engaged: research 43–49; as sociopolitical practice 49–53
Every Child Achieves Act of 2015 Title I 7–8

feminist anthropology 41
Le Fetuao Samoan Language Center 75
Fine, M. 35–36
France 95
Fraser, Nancy 108
freedom of speech 26
Freire, P. 29, 49–53
French language and culture 5
funds of knowledge 98–99

García, O. 48
Germany 8
globalization. *see* neoliberalism
Google Translate 87

Harvey, D. 22–23
Harvey, J. 33
Hawai'i 6–7, 52; neoliberal resistance in 71–75
Hawley, M. K. 102
hegemonic language ideologies 32–38
hegemony, Gramsci's theory of 14–15
Helot, C. 93, 94
hip-hop 9
historical-structural approach, vs. neoclassical approach 2–3
How to Conduct a Community Self-Survey of Civil Rights (Wormser and Selltiz 1951) 40
human welfare 61
Hymes, D. 41

identity investment 91–93
ideological analyses, exploration of 28–29
ideologies: defined 17; historical construction of 14–16; as historical objects 18–19; mother-tongue ideology 20; and multilingualism 17–20
immigrants 87
India 24–25, 54, 100
indigenous critical praxis 99

inequality, linguistic and educational 81–82
International Monetary Fund 23, 26
International Organization for Migration 8

Ka Papahana Kaiapuni (Hawaiian Language Immersion Program) 72
language education policy, alternatives 60
language ideologies. *see* ideologies
language orientations, Ruiz's conceptualization of 28
language policies, politics and processes of 5
language policies and planning (LPP) 39, 47
language policies and practices: historical construction of 14–16; and ideological analyses 28–29
Language Policies in Education: Critical Issues (Tollefson 2013) 47
language policy, right to 107–113
Lefebvre, Henri 107
Li, W. 48, 82, 86
liberating pedagogy 51
Lin, A. M. Y. 58
linguistic democracy, principle of 2
linguistic inequality, addressing 81–82
literacy 26
Little (Treuer 1995) 4
Luxembourg 6
Luxembourgish 29

Mapp, Karen 77
Martin Luther King Jr. Elementary School v. Ann Arbor Board of Education 2
A Match on Dry Grass: Community Organizing as a Catalyst for School Reform (Warren & Mapp 2011) 77
Mathers, A. 49
Max, C. 76
McCarty, T. 29, 39–40
McNally, D. 27
Mead, Margaret 40
Micronesia 75
minoritized language: erasure of 20–21; use of term 2
monoglossic ideologies 96
mother-tongue ideology 20. *see also* ideologies
multicompetence 85, 93–94

multilingual language awareness (MLA) 96
multilingual policies and practices 76–77, 93–94; complementary schools 85
multilingualism: erasure of 20–21; and ideologies 17–20; recognition of 9–10
multimedia resources 87

national language policies 5
Navajo people 44
neoclassical approach, vs. historical-structural approach 2–3
neoliberal fatalism 50
neoliberalism 22–27
Nepal 6, 24, 31–32, 56–57; ideological transformation in 63–71
Nicaragua 25
No Child Left Behind initiative 6, 51, 53, 74
Novelli, M. 49

objectivity, challenging the notion of 33
O'Laoire, M. 94

Pacific Islanders 7
Pakistan 59
parents, engagement of 102–104
Parents Involvement in Quality Education 101–102
participatory action research (PAR) approach 32–35, 46
participatory policy-making 53–55
Partners for Urban Knowledge Action and Research (PUKAR) 54
pedagogy of hope 94, 106
Pedagogy of the Oppressed (Freire 1970) 29, 49–53
pedagogy of the possible 94–95
Philippines 25, 100
Phyak, P. 63–71
Pidgin 71
plurilingual educational practices 87, 95, 96
policy activism 10–11
policy advocacy 9–10
policy-making, participatory 53–55
political decision-making, guiding principles 2–4
Portante, D. 76
poverty 26
praxis 52
private schools 64. *see also* schools
public schools, in the United States 30

Pueblo youth 31
Puerto Rican children 44

Quechua communities 44

racial oppression 26–27
raciolinguistic ideology 27
Reagan, Ronald 22
refugee migration 5, 8
Reinventing Anthropology (Hymes 1969) 41
resistance, planning 60–62
Resisting Linguistic Imperialism in English Language Teaching (Canagarajah 1999) 58
right to language policy 107–113
Roberts, R. A. 35–36
Rockford Bullying Study and Polling for Justice (Stoudt et al. 2011) 34–35
Rockwell, R. E. 102

School Sector Reform Program and Highe Education Project 63
schools: alternative global/local programs 77–78; effective schooling 63; private schools 64; public schools 30
Selltiz, C. 40
Shohamy, E. 45
social justice 29–32, 86–91
social reproduction, marketing of 61
Solomon Islands 55
South Africa 25, 90
South Korea 26
Spanish heritage language (SHL) speakers 97–98
structure of competition, notion of 26
students 48
Studies of Heritage and Academic Languages and Literacies (SHALL) program 72
subaltern counterpublics 9
Syrian refugees 8

teachers 48; supporting 88–90, 97
terrorist attacks, effects of 8
Thatcher, Margaret 22
third space 89
Tollefson, J. W. 9, 47, 112
Torre, M. E. 35–36
translanguaging 10, 48, 76, 82–86
Treuer, David 4

Ubuntu 90
UN Development Program (UNDP) 63
UN High Commissioner for Refugees 8
United States 87; *Common Core Standards* mandate 6, 53, 74, 76; *No Child Left Behind* initiative 6, 51, 53, 74; public schools 30
Urdu 59

Warren, M. R. 77

words, loss of 4
World Bank 23, 26, 63
world-system theory 25
Wormser, M. H. 40

Young, A. S. 93

Zhu, H. 82, 86

Taylor & Francis eBooks

Helping you to choose the right eBooks for your Library

Add Routledge titles to your library's digital collection today. Taylor and Francis ebooks contains over 50,000 titles in the Humanities, Social Sciences, Behavioural Sciences, Built Environment and Law.

Choose from a range of subject packages or create your own!

Benefits for you
- Free MARC records
- COUNTER-compliant usage statistics
- Flexible purchase and pricing options
- All titles DRM-free.

Benefits for your user
- Off-site, anytime access via Athens or referring URL
- Print or copy pages or chapters
- Full content search
- Bookmark, highlight and annotate text
- Access to thousands of pages of quality research at the click of a button.

REQUEST YOUR FREE INSTITUTIONAL TRIAL TODAY | **Free Trials Available** We offer free trials to qualifying academic, corporate and government customers.

eCollections – Choose from over 30 subject eCollections, including:

Archaeology	Language Learning
Architecture	Law
Asian Studies	Literature
Business & Management	Media & Communication
Classical Studies	Middle East Studies
Construction	Music
Creative & Media Arts	Philosophy
Criminology & Criminal Justice	Planning
Economics	Politics
Education	Psychology & Mental Health
Energy	Religion
Engineering	Security
English Language & Linguistics	Social Work
Environment & Sustainability	Sociology
Geography	Sport
Health Studies	Theatre & Performance
History	Tourism, Hospitality & Events

For more information, pricing enquiries or to order a free trial, please contact your local sales team:
www.tandfebooks.com/page/sales

Routledge Taylor & Francis Group | The home of Routledge books

www.tandfebooks.com